Needlecraft Treasury
from Adalee Winter

Needlecraft Treasury
from Adalee Winter

Oxmoor House, Inc., Birmingham

Copyright© 1979 by Oxmoor House, Inc.
Book Division of The Progressive Farmer Company
Publisher of *Southern Living*®, *Progressive Farmer*®, and
  Decorating & Craft Ideas® magazines.
P.O. Box 2463, Birmingham, Alabama 35202

Eugene Butler	Chairman of the Board
Emory Cunningham	President and Publisher
Vernon Owens, Jr.	Senior Vice President
Roger McGuire	Executive Vice President

Conceived, edited and published by Oxmoor House, Inc.,
under the direction of:

Don Logan	Vice President and General Manager
Gary McCalla	Editor, *Southern Living*
John Logue	Editor-in-Chief
Mary Elizabeth Johnson	Senior Editor, Crafts
Candace N. Conard	Editor, Crafts
Mary Jo Sherrill	Associate Editor, Crafts
Jerry Higdon	Production Manager
Mary Jean Haddin	Copy Chief

Needlecraft Treasury from Adalee Winter

Editor: Candace N. Conard
Book Design and Photography: Steve Logan
Illustrator: Don K. Smith
Stitching of projects for photography: Linda Clarke, Eliza-
  beth Findlay, Gayle Garrittson, Jean Gordon, Fran
  Gregg, Lois Kramer, Connie Lee, Ruth Winter, Terri
  Winter.

Southern Living® and *Progressive Farmer*® are federally
registered trademarks belonging to The Progressive
Farmer Company. *Decorating & Craft Ideas*® is a federally registered trademark belonging to Southern Living,
Inc.

Library of Congress Catalog Number: 79-83708
ISBN: 0-8487-0499-1

Manufactured in the United States of America
First Printing 1979

Contents

Introduction 6

Butterflies & Birds 9

Flower Garden 27

Kids' Stuff 47

Celebrations.................................. 59

Symbols of Worship 81

Fun & Games.................................. 103

Animal Menagerie............................ 113

Around the World 129

Serendipity 139

A to Z... 155

Appendix 174

Index 192

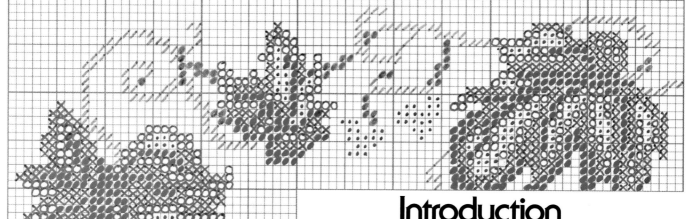

Introduction

My first chart drawn for needlework was a happy inspiration. A very dear friend, Clara Buchanan, taught me to do cross stitch on ravel-out canvas by following a chart. At that time, there were few graph charts available, and Clara often complained that she had used the few DMC booklets in print and one alphabet chart that had been passed around so often that she was tired of all of the designs. So when I wanted to send her a particularly meaningful present, I drew a chart of wildflowers for her to cross stitch. She loved it!

When the chart was published in a magazine, I began to get requests for *needlepoint* charts. My reaction was "What is needlepoint?" A quick bit of research showed needlepoint to be very popular, but in the 1960s, it was really more a matter of filling in background stitches around preworked designs of cabbages, roses, fruits, birds, musical instruments, and other Victorian designs.

Today's stitchers are reaching out for more modern, more original, and more personal designs—more and better ways to express a needleworker's expertise and creativity. I wondered why needlepoint could not be worked from graph charts, so I drew one or two, using my

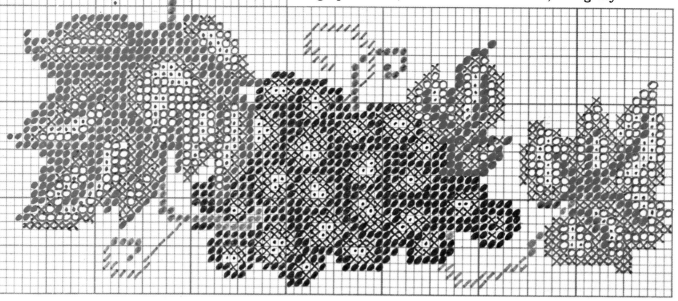

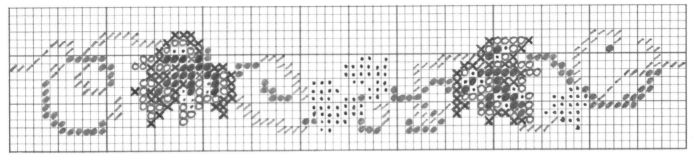

wildflower designs, and then I stitched them up.

The design areas worked up rather well, except that the flower stems that slanted from lower right to upper left on the chart looked like separated dots rather than a continous line when I worked them, due to the slant of the needlepoint stitch. I also made the mistake of working the background in a half-cross stitch (all that the local needlework shop had time to teach me), so the end result was awful.

I know now that the only acceptable background stitch is basketweave or a pattern stitch, and that basketweave is also best in large areas of the design. I framed my first attempt at needlepoint and have it hanging on my office wall to remind me of how bad I once was, and how much I have learned since that time.

After my first attempts at creating a needlework chart, I spent nine years of training in graph chart designing. I was flooded with requests for charted designs, nearly always for needlepoint. Charted designs of houses, pets, people, school symbols, and other more unexpected requests such as one for a chart of a slobbering wolf pack, a Scotsman in a plaid kilt, and a Mac truck, all came to my drawing table.

My first reaction often was "I can't do that." But my youngest son believed that a mother could do anything; my husband's attitude was "Why not?" and I found I simply could not resist a challenge. The end result was that, while I might not always like the topics I am asked to design a chart for, I have come to believe that any picture or quotation can be charted for needlework.

Everywhere I look now, I see things that I would like to translate into needlework designs. Some of the earlier custom designs have gone into my books. Other sources of design ideas have been songs; photographs; religious symbols; and personal hobbies such as wildflowers, seashells, and playing bridge.

One of the most exciting things about designing needlework charts is visualizing how they can be used once they are "stitched up." For many years, needleworkers either turned their creations into pillows or framed them to hang on their walls. The designs in my book can be used in so many more varied ways. Cross stitch a border of wildflowers on your kitchen curtains; needlepoint my Indian designs into a belt or a guitar strap; or work with your church guild to needlepoint religious symbols for kneeling cushions or alter cloths.

Eight of my bird designs were created specifically for dining room chair seats; a bright children's design could work beautifully in needlepoint as a scrap book or baby album cover. Surprise a new bride with a needlepoint mat for her wedding announcement. Or why not enlarge the signs of the zodiac and make a rug for your teenager? I've made purses out of some of my designs, and a friend used the zodiac signs as a clock face.

Don't be afraid to use only portions of a chart. Select a border design from one chapter and team it with a main design from another, or work the smaller bird designs into some of the flower patterns. I know that the stitching woman in the Saint Peter design on page 174

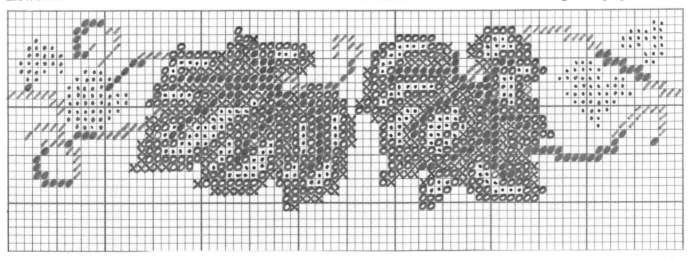

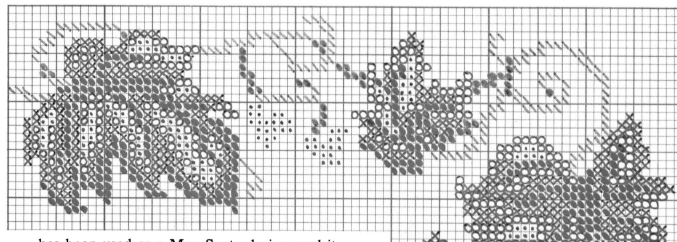

has been used as a Mrs. Santa design, and it works beautifully. The possibilities are endless; you are limited only by your imagination.

The Appendix is full of valuable information to acquaint the novice with cross stitch and needlepoint techniques and to encourage experienced needleworkers to try their hand at some of the more decorative stitches. The Appendix also discusses how to work from a charted design, blocking needlework, enlarging patterns, following a stitch diagram, plus a beautifully illustrated stitch dictionary.

I've tried to include something for everyone in my *Treasury,* from simple, basic designs for beginners to complicated patterns with intricate shading for more advanced stitchers.

Sometimes I receive a note from a stranger saying, "I use your book more than any other I own." And fairly often I see an almost worn out copy of one of my books. These things mean more to me than any number of awards. The important part of my life has been being a good wife and a good mother. But I take special joy from the fact that I may have given numbers of people, most of whom I will never meet, some pleasure in stitching from my designs. I know I have truly enjoyed drawing them.

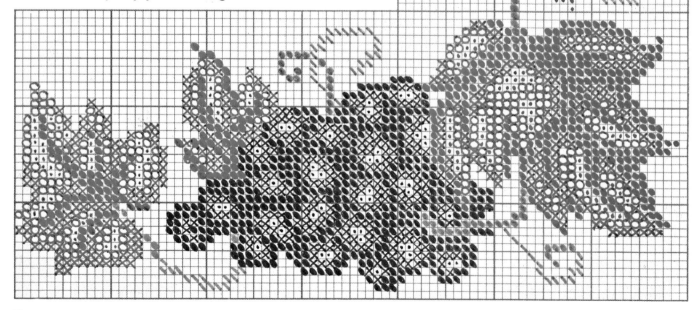

Butterflies & Birds

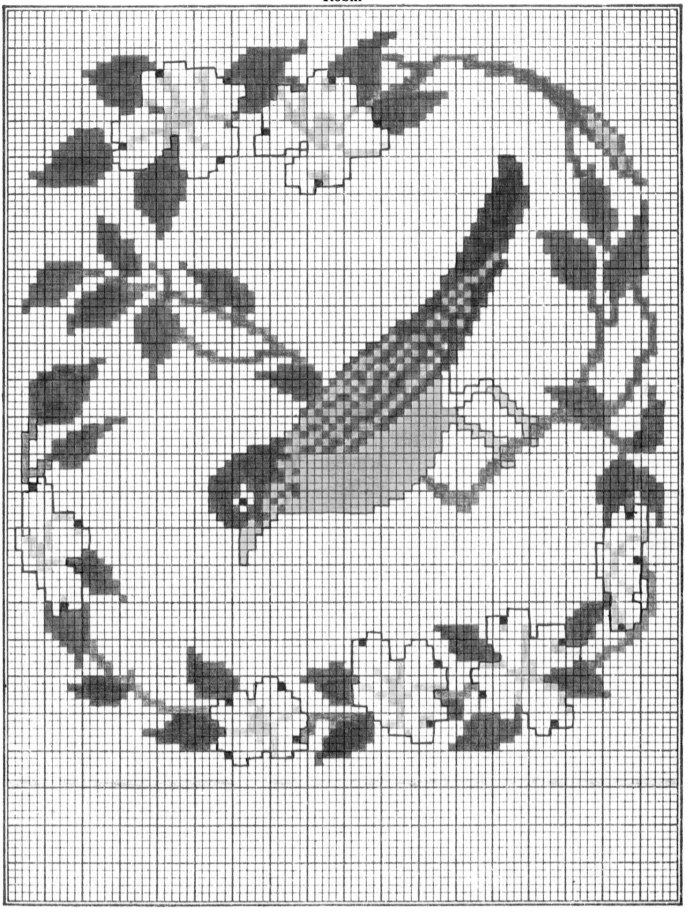

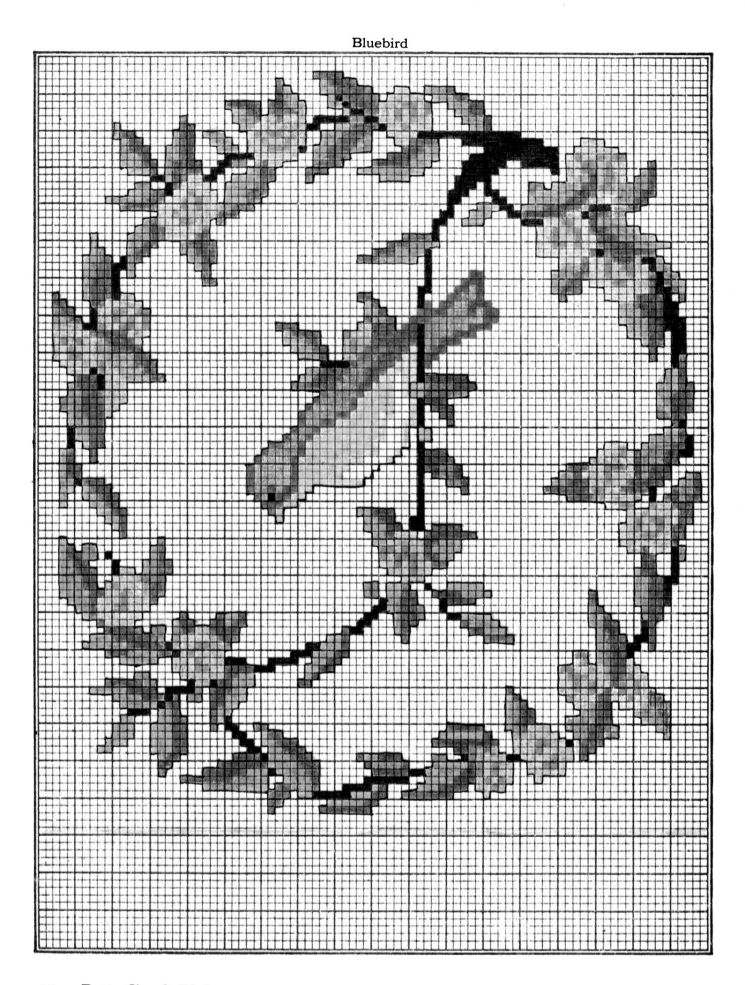

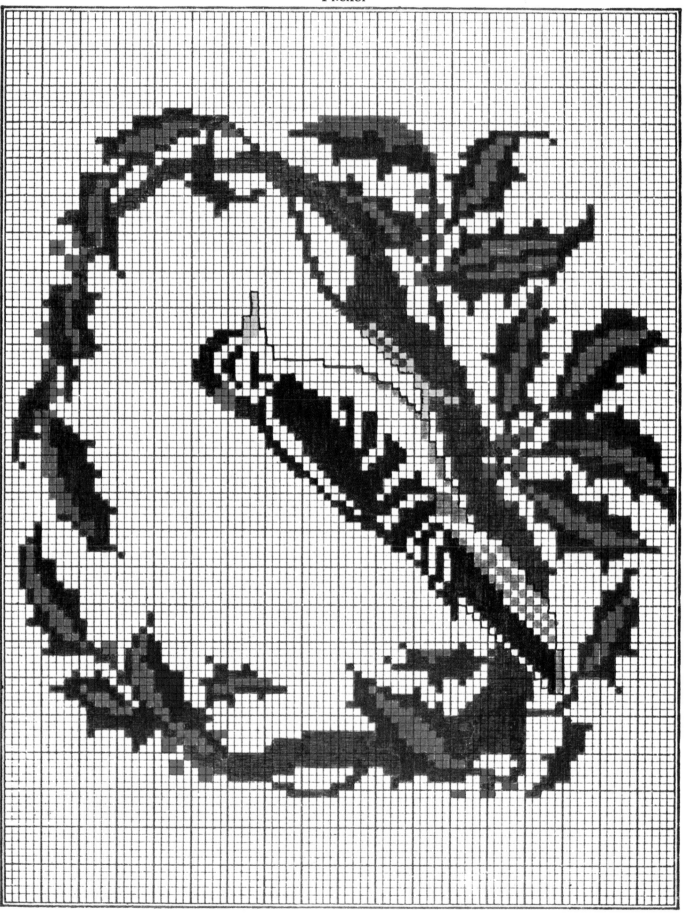

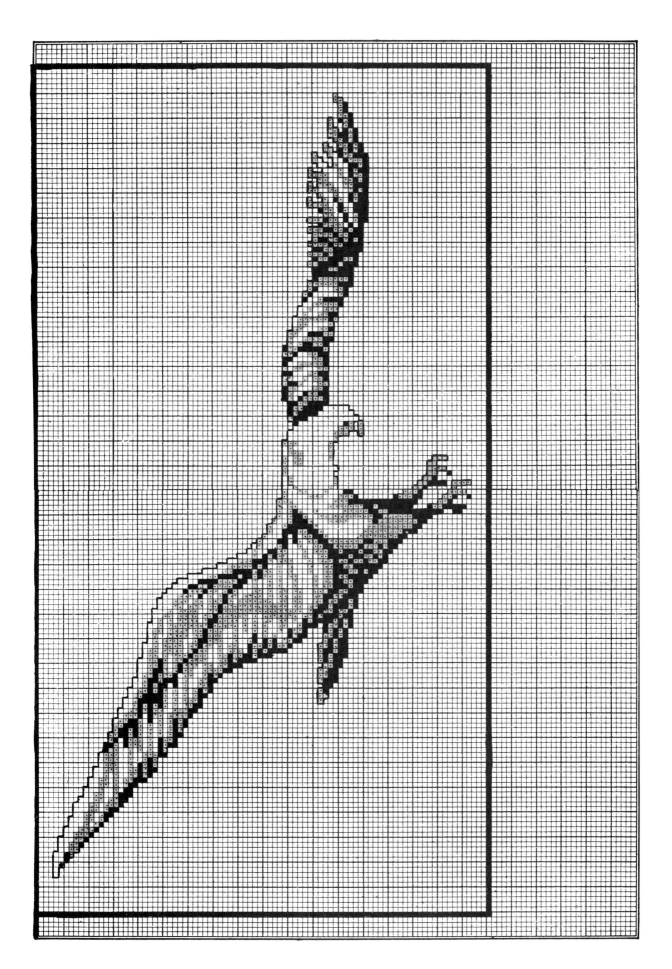

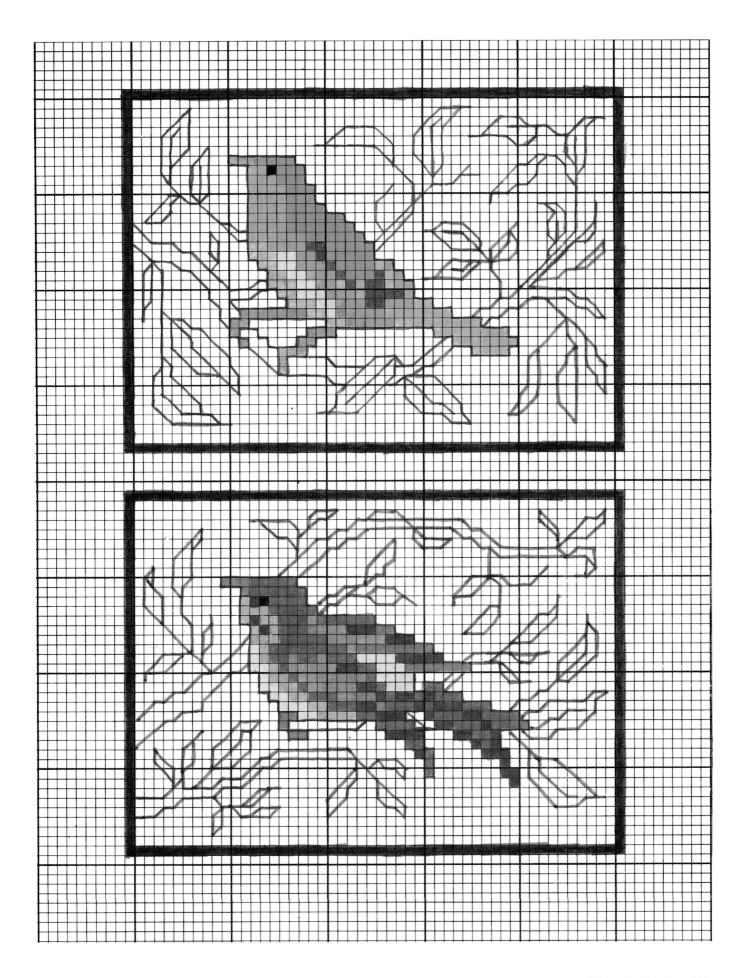

26   Butterflies & Birds

Flower Garden

Yellow Jessamine

• light yellow	l light rust	✗ green
⟍ yellow	O pale green	■ dark green
+ dark yellow	< light green	— yellow green

Wild Man of the Earth
• white   O rose   ■ pale yellow green   \ green
∧ pale rose   X dark rose   / light yellow green   V dark green

INITIALS

- white
o pale grey
/ light grey
N tan
● brown
C pale green
↖ light green
II green
✕ dark green
Y yellow

Purple Joe-Pye Weed
X purple
· light purple
/ light green
— green
+ dark green
V light olive green
\ olive green

Lotus

Daisy

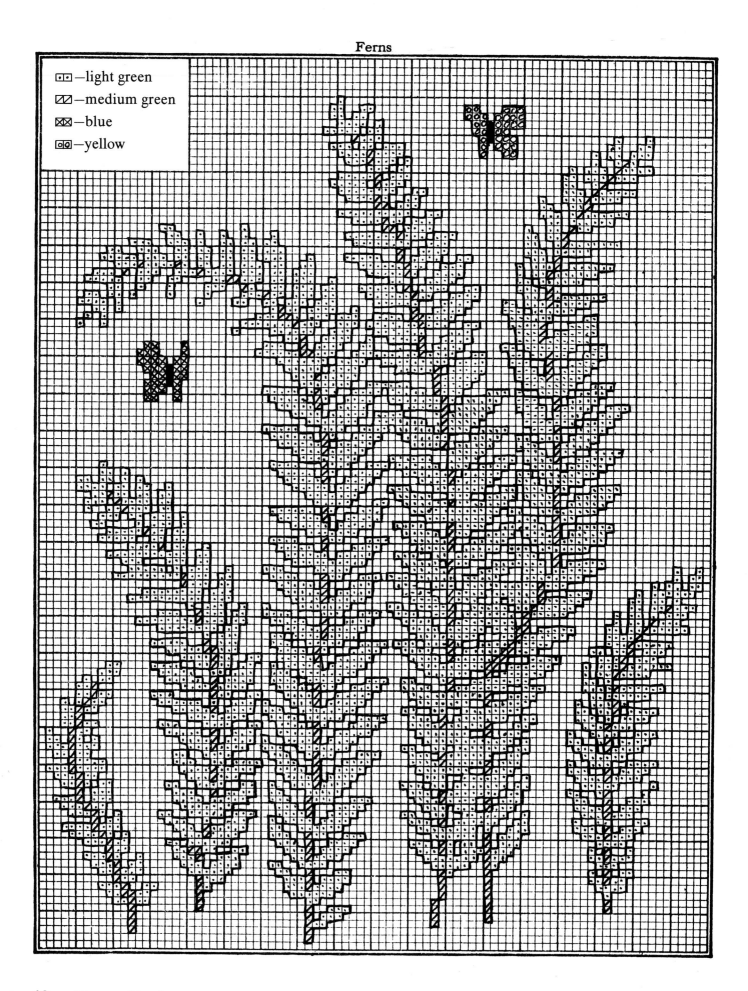

Red Clover
- · light red purple
- O red purple
- / light blue green
- — blue green
- X dark blue green
- V grey green
- ∧ dark grey green

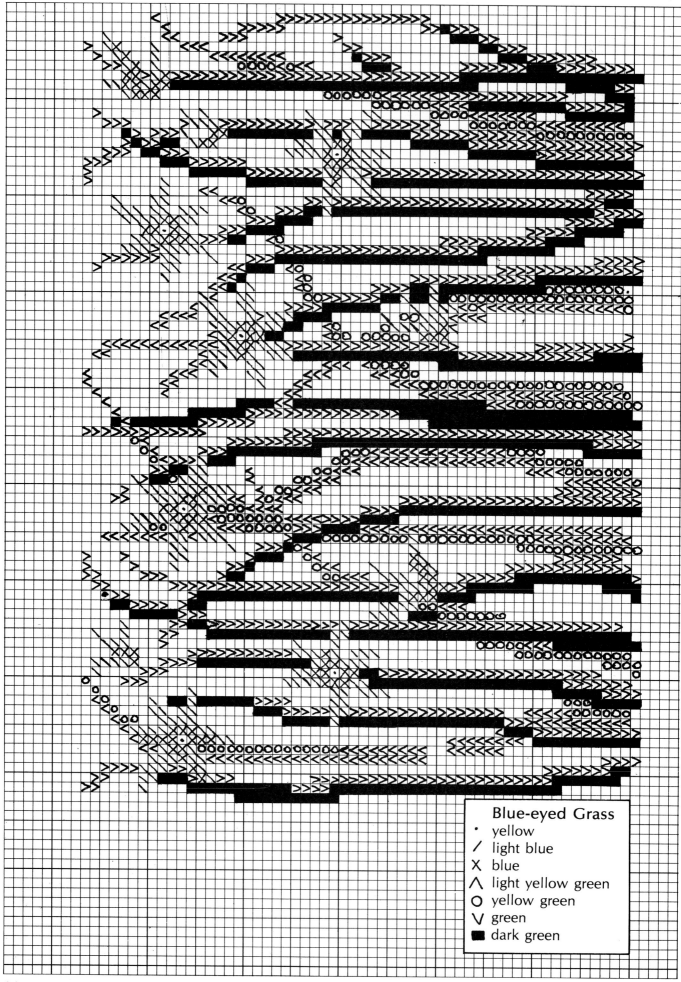

Blue-eyed Grass

- • yellow
- / light blue
- X blue
- ∧ light yellow green
- O yellow green
- V green
- ■ dark green

Orange Milkwort

- ■ orange
- ∧ dark orange
- • light yellow green
- / yellow green
- × olive green
- ○ dark olive green

Kids' Stuff

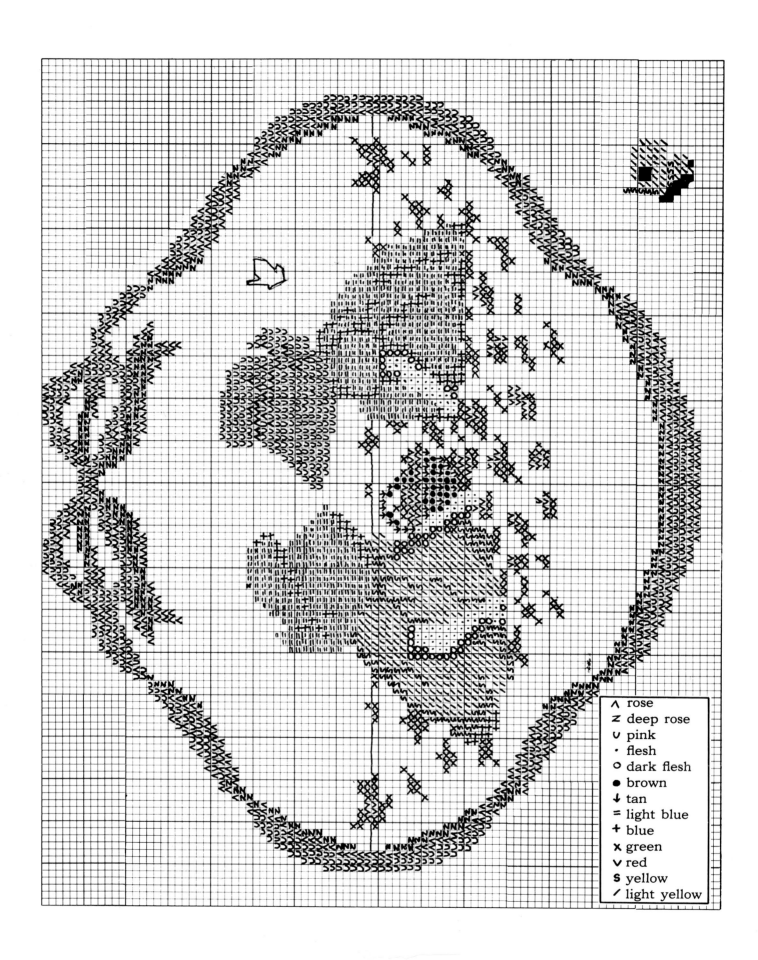

∧ rose
z deep rose
∨ pink
· flesh
○ dark flesh
● brown
↓ tan
= light blue
+ blue
x green
v red
s yellow
∕ light yellow

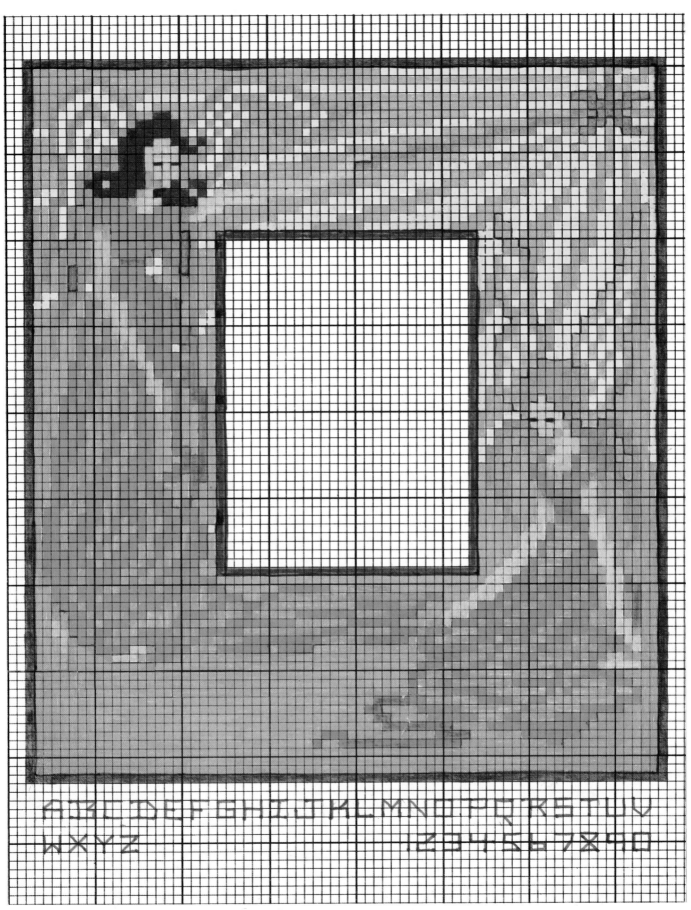

Write child's name and birth date with backstitching
in lower left corner of frame.

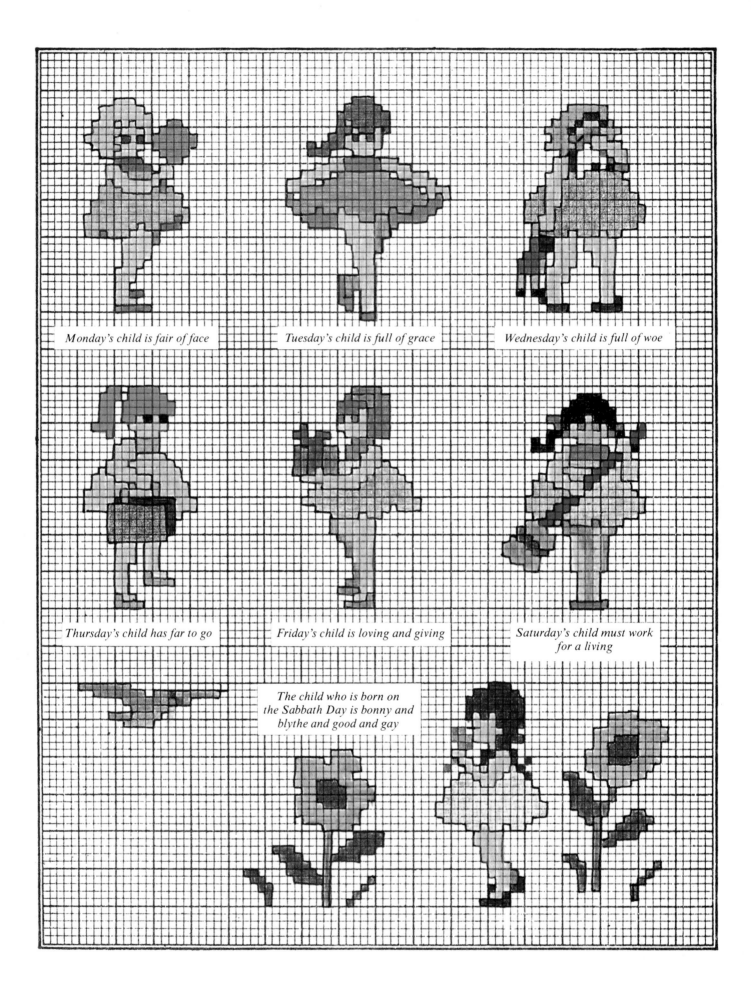

Monday's child is fair of face

Tuesday's child is full of grace

Wednesday's child is full of woe

Thursday's child has far to go

Friday's child is loving and giving

Saturday's child must work for a living

The child who is born on the Sabbath Day is bonny and blythe and good and gay

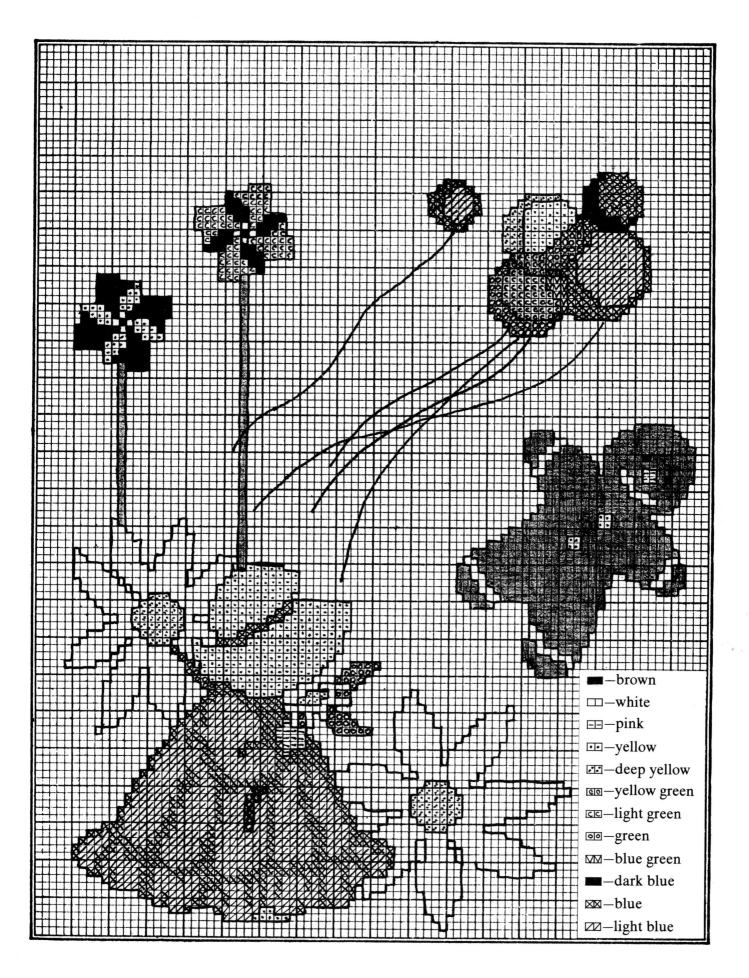

■ —brown
⊡ —white
⊞ —pink
⊡ —yellow
⊠ —deep yellow
⊡ —yellow green
⊡ —light green
⊡ —green
⋈ —blue green
■ —dark blue
⊠ —blue
⧄ —light blue

black — black   □ — red
□ — white   ■ — dark flesh
■ — grey   ■ — light flesh

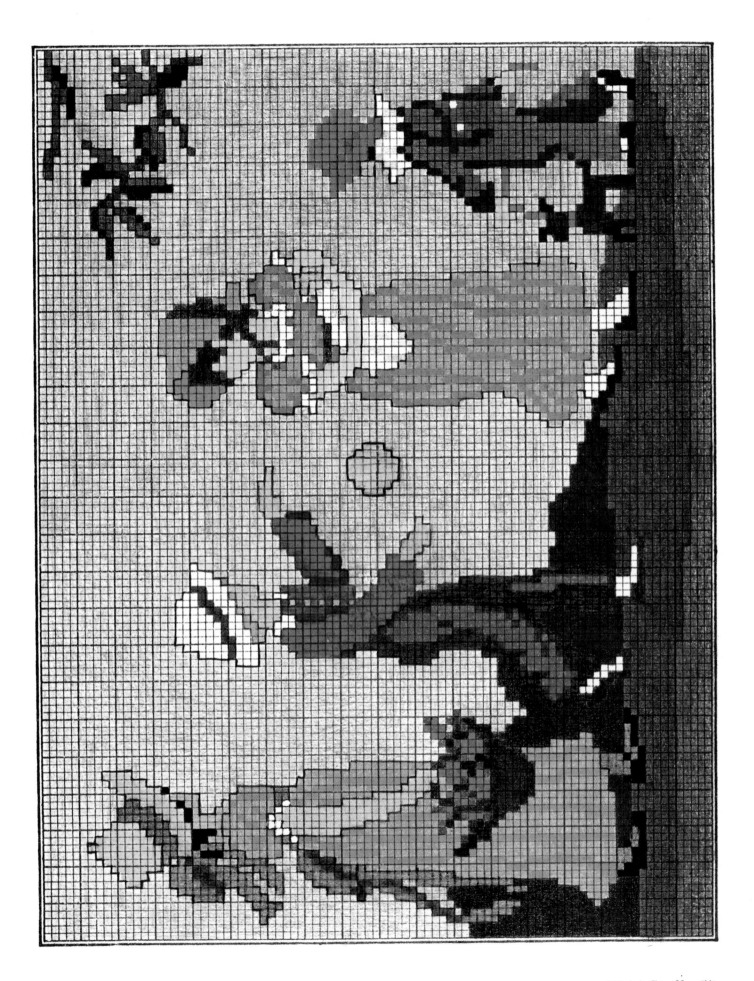

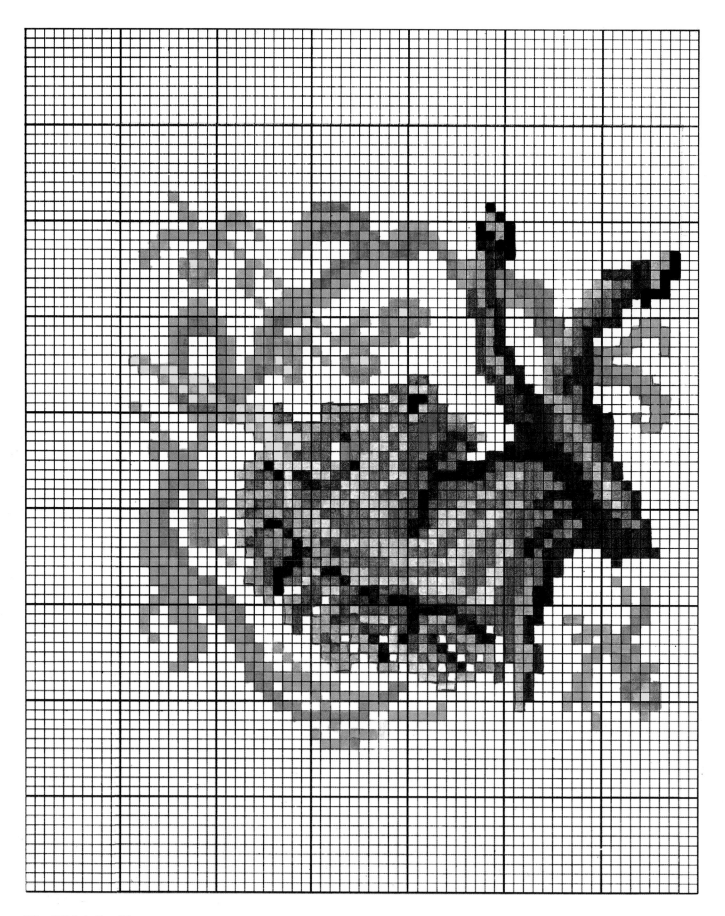

58 Kids' Stuff

Celebrations

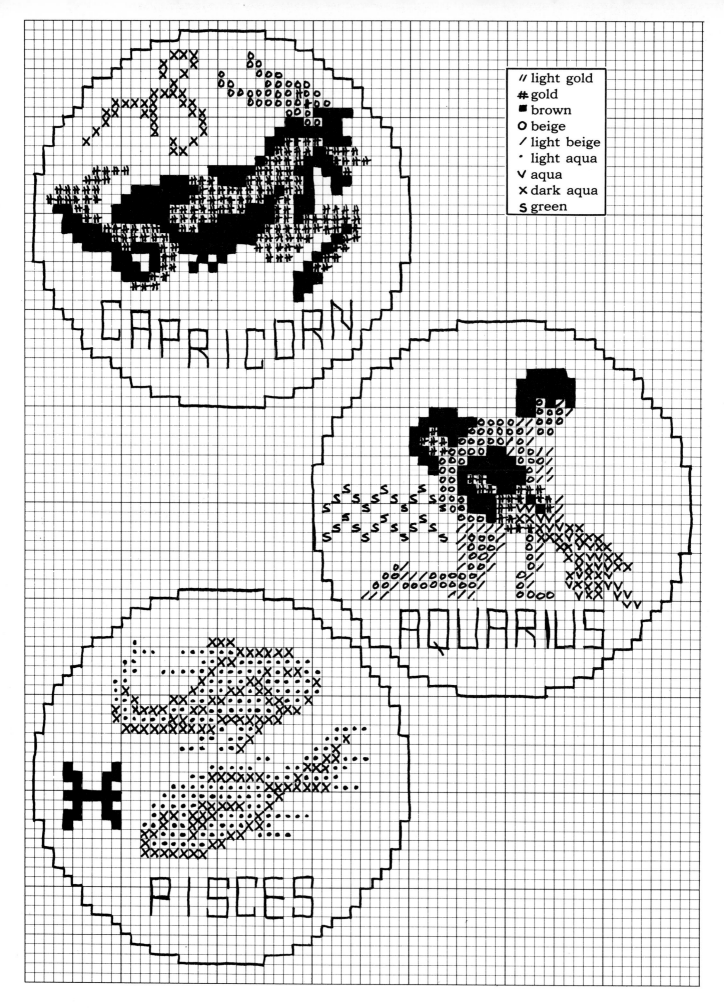

Legend:
- // light gold
- # gold
- ■ brown
- O beige
- / light beige
- • light aqua
- V aqua
- X dark aqua
- S green

CAPRICORN

AQUARIUS

PISCES

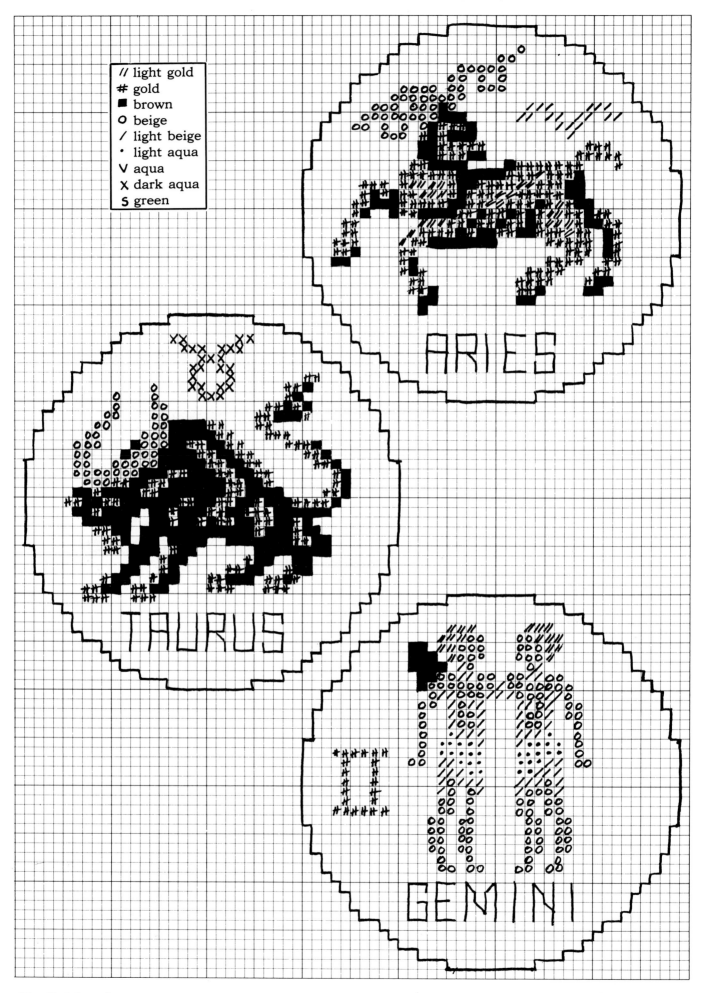

Legend:
// light gold
gold
■ brown
O beige
/ light beige
· light aqua
V aqua
X dark aqua
S green

ARIES

TAURUS

GEMINI

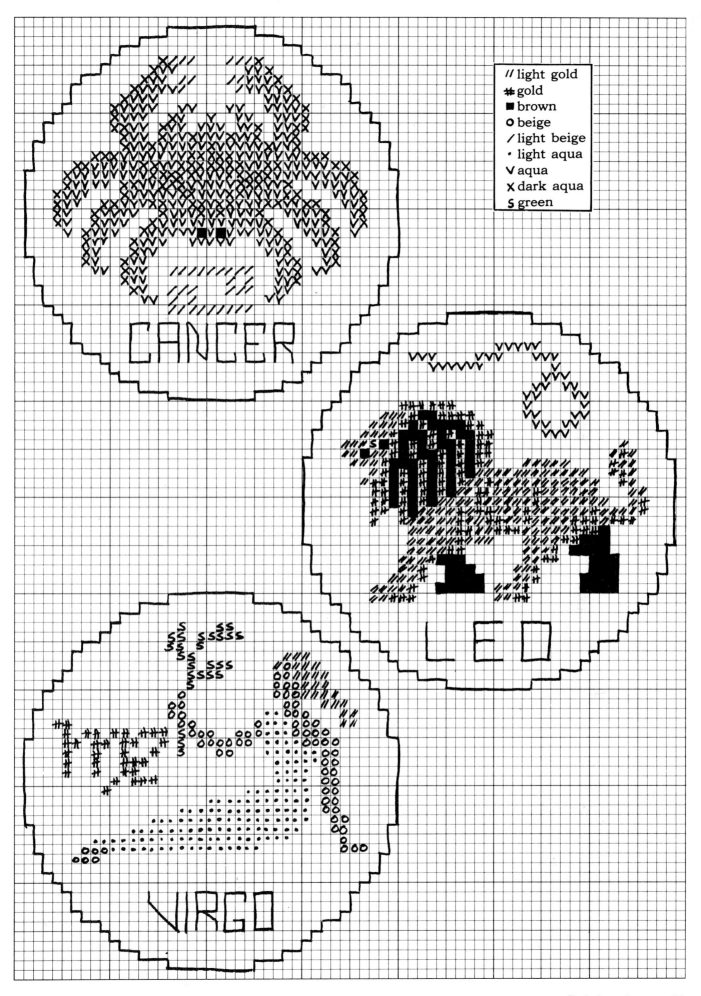

CANCER

LEO

VIRGO

// light gold
\# gold
■ brown
O beige
/ light beige
• light aqua
V aqua
X dark aqua
S green

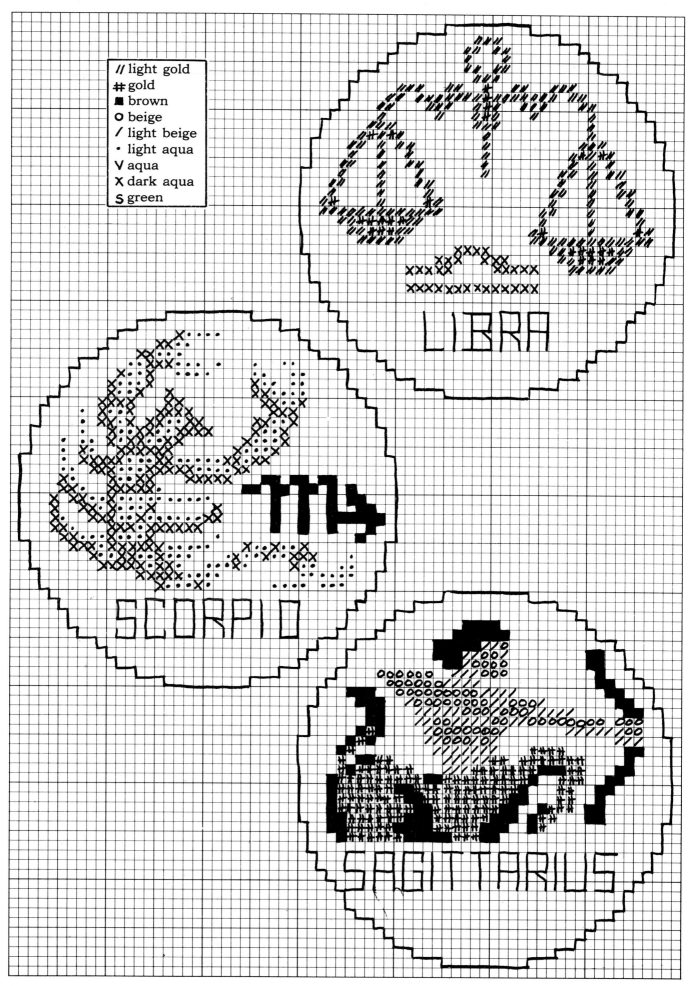

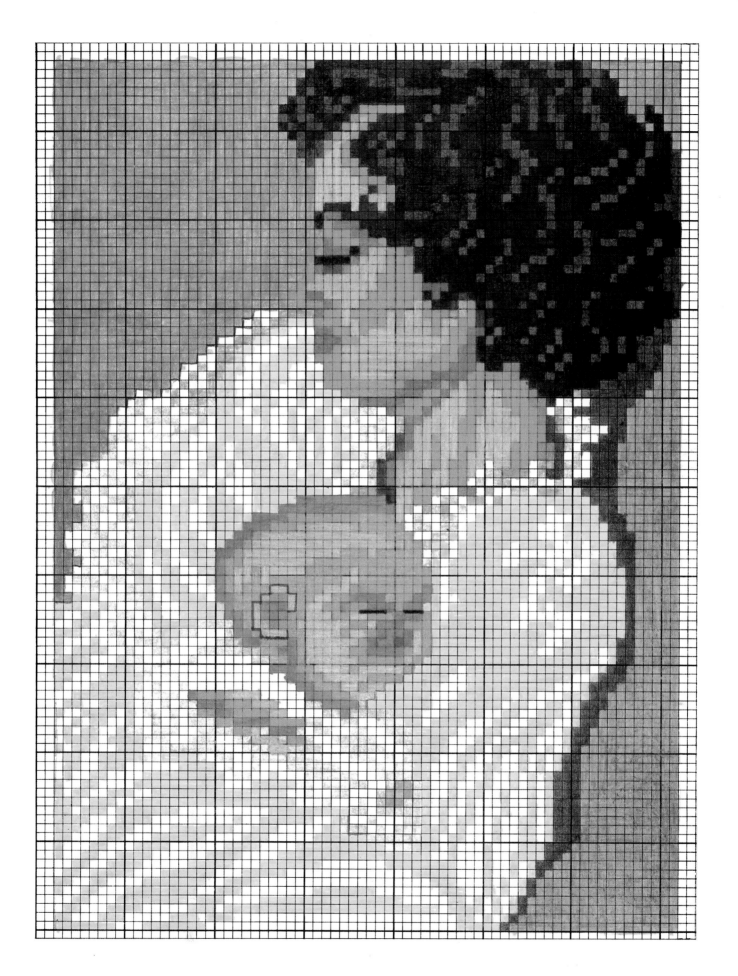

· pale yellow, blue, gold or other background color   ⊠ blue

⊙ flesh   ☐ white

⊠ black   backstitching—black

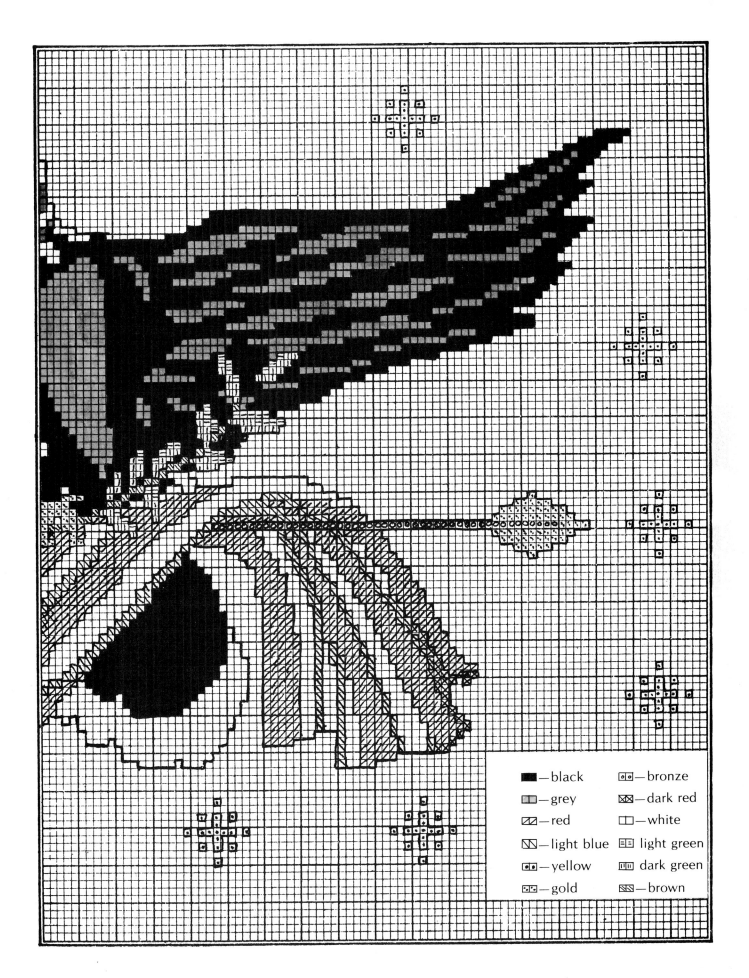

■ —black		▦ —bronze
▤ —grey		⊠ —dark red
▨ —red		⊞ —white
⊠ —light blue		⊞ —light green
⊡ —yellow		⊞ —dark green
⊡ —gold		▧ —brown

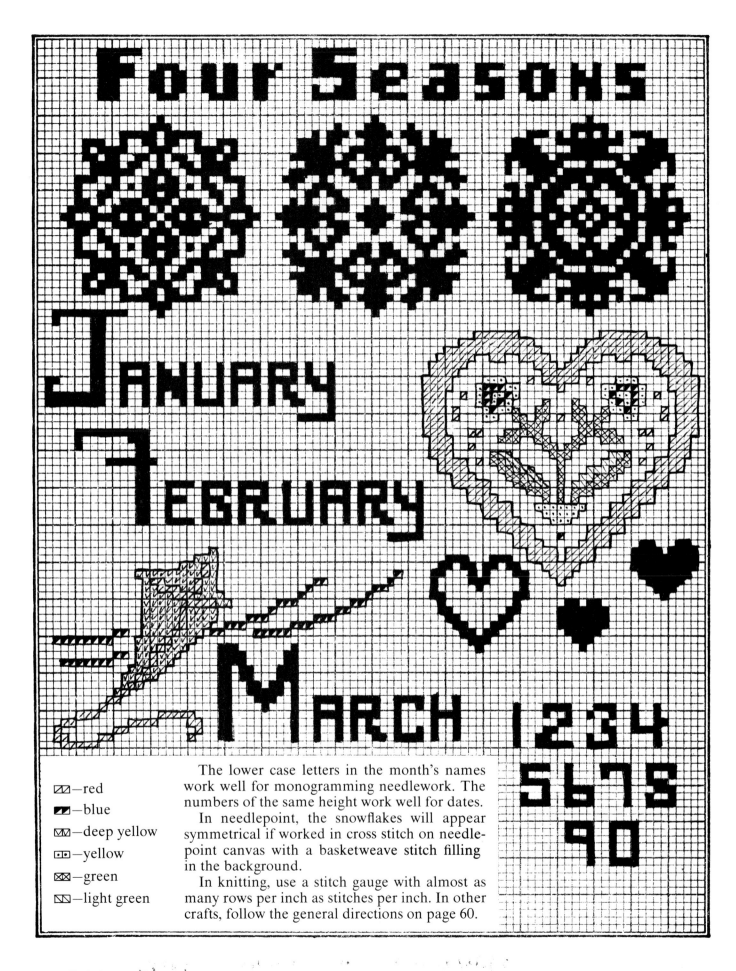

Four Seasons

January

February

March

1 2 3 4
5 6 7 8
9 0

☑☑—red
☑☑—blue
☑☑—deep yellow
☑☑—yellow
☑☑—green
☑☑—light green

The lower case letters in the month's names work well for monogramming needlework. The numbers of the same height work well for dates.

In needlepoint, the snowflakes will appear symmetrical if worked in cross stitch on needlepoint canvas with a basketweave stitch filling in the background.

In knitting, use a stitch gauge with almost as many rows per inch as stitches per inch. In other crafts, follow the general directions on page 60.

slit

fold line

slit

fold line

fold line

Cut
Out

slit

fold line

slit

Symbols of Worship

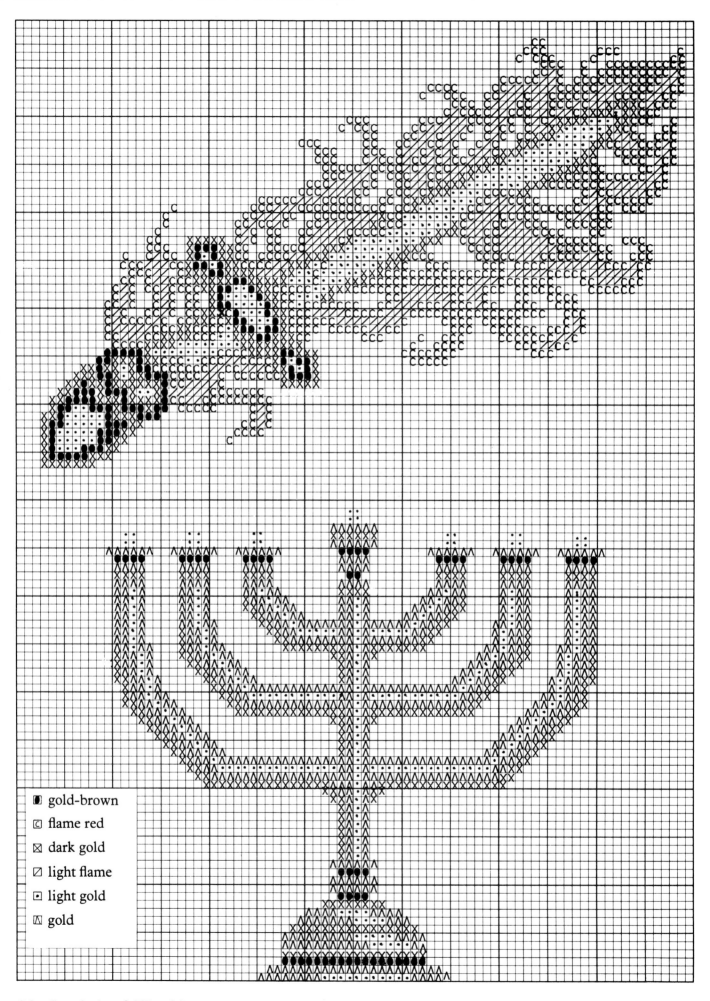

■ gold-brown

ᶜ flame red

⊠ dark gold

⊿ light flame

· light gold

⋀ gold

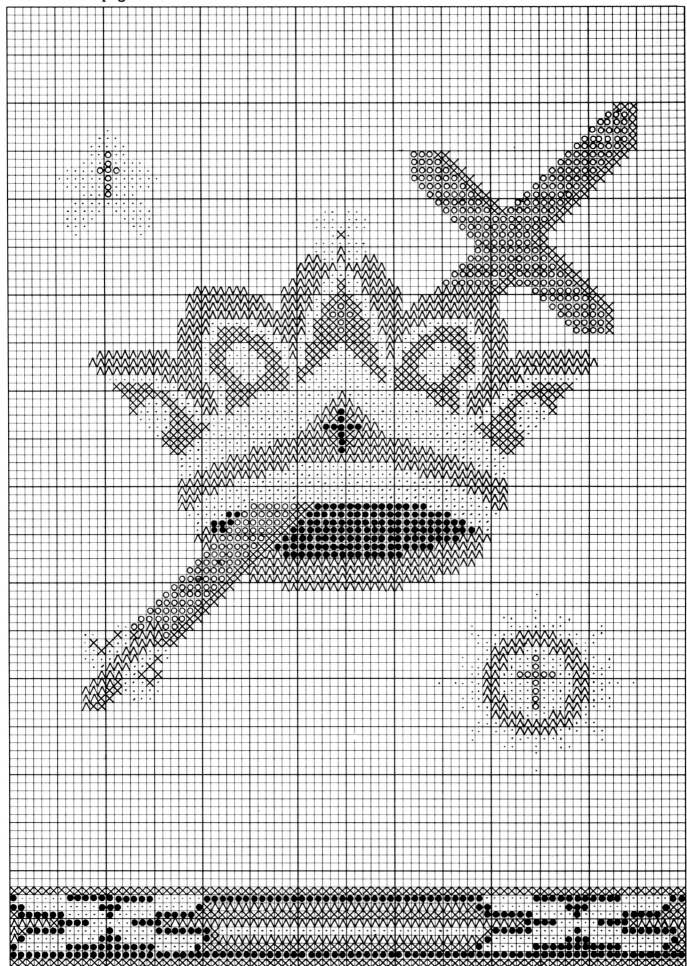

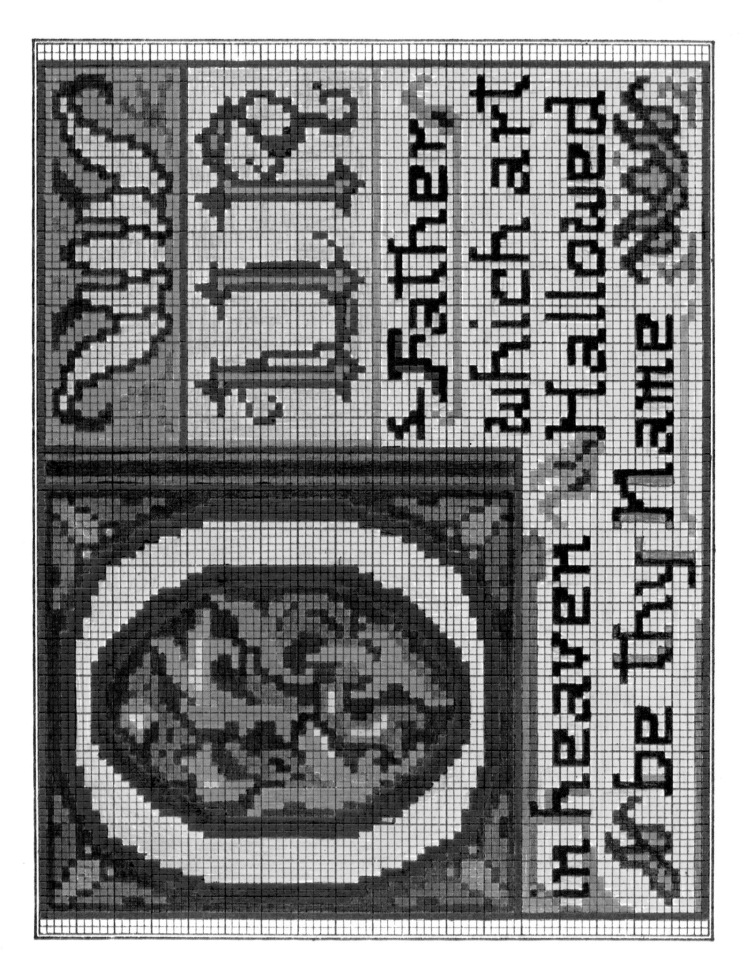

Color Coding for pages 89, 90, 91

⊠ deep gold   ⊠ green

⧄ gold   ⊞ red

⊡ white or pale gold

◩ purple   Suggested background colors: red, green, purple and white.

92 Symbols of Worship

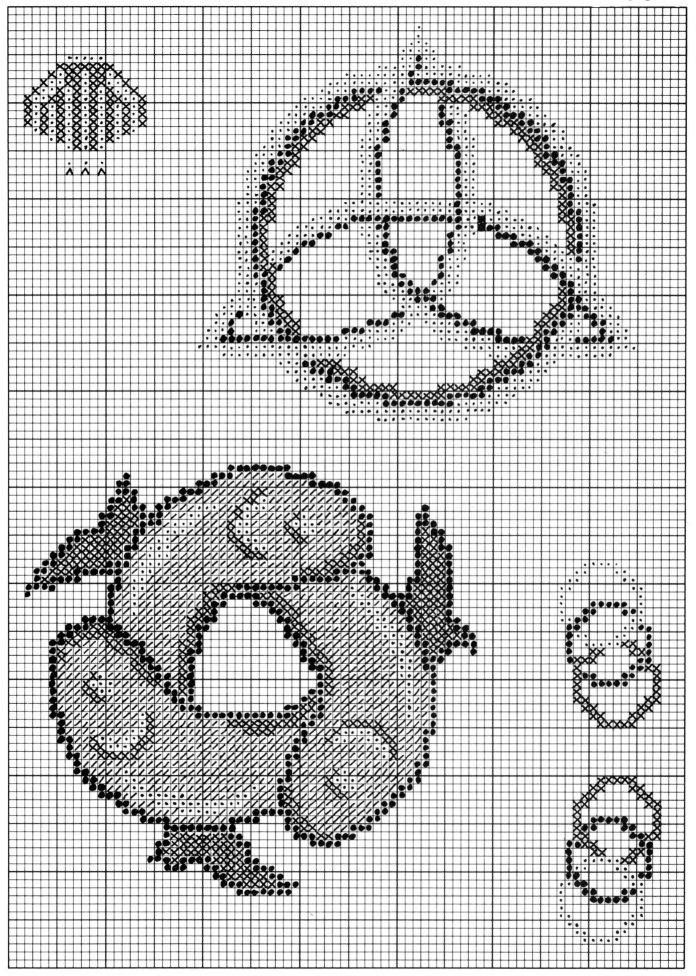

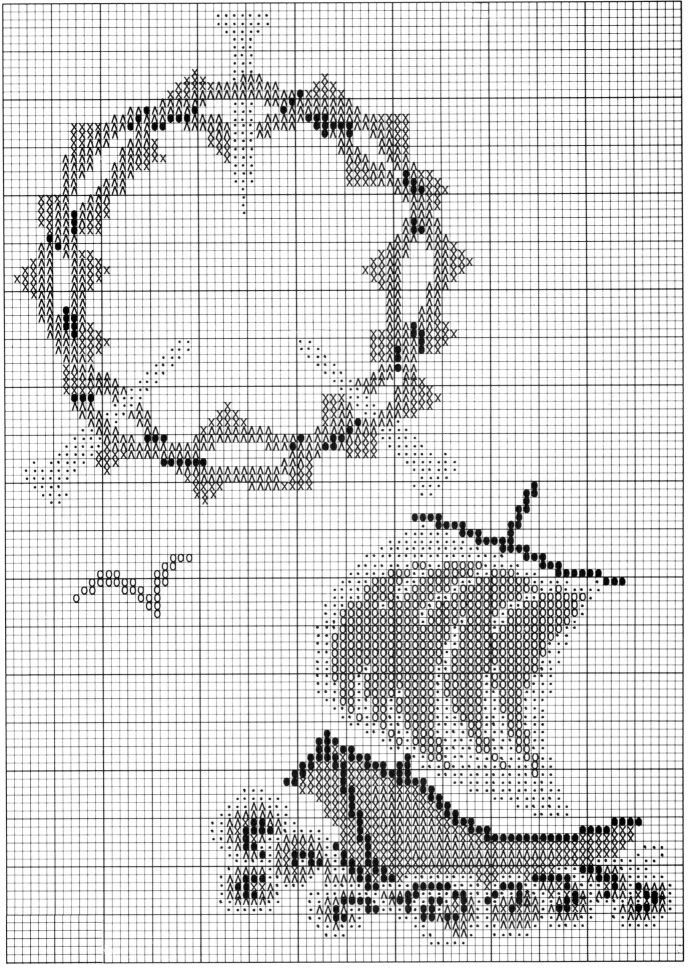

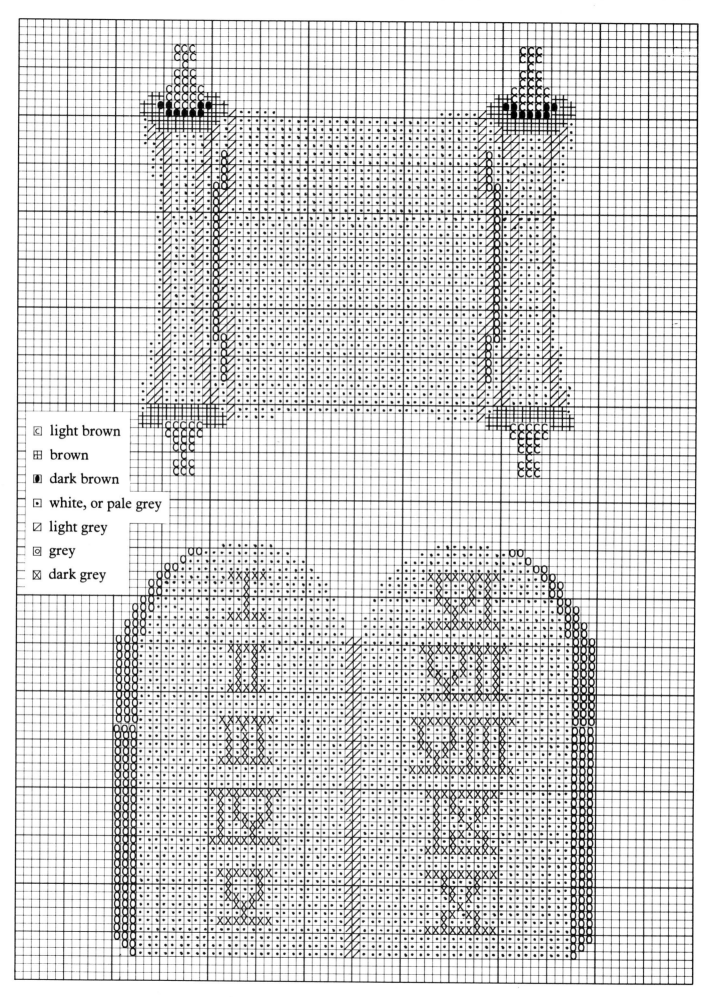

light brown

brown

dark brown

white, or pale grey

light grey

grey

dark grey

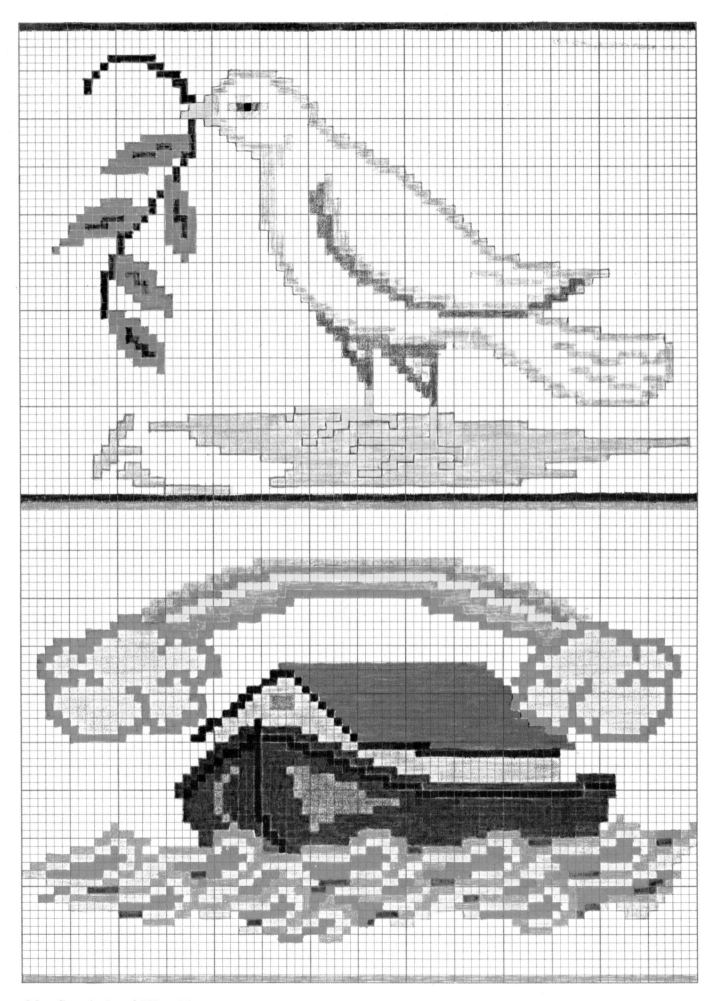

98 Symbols of Worship

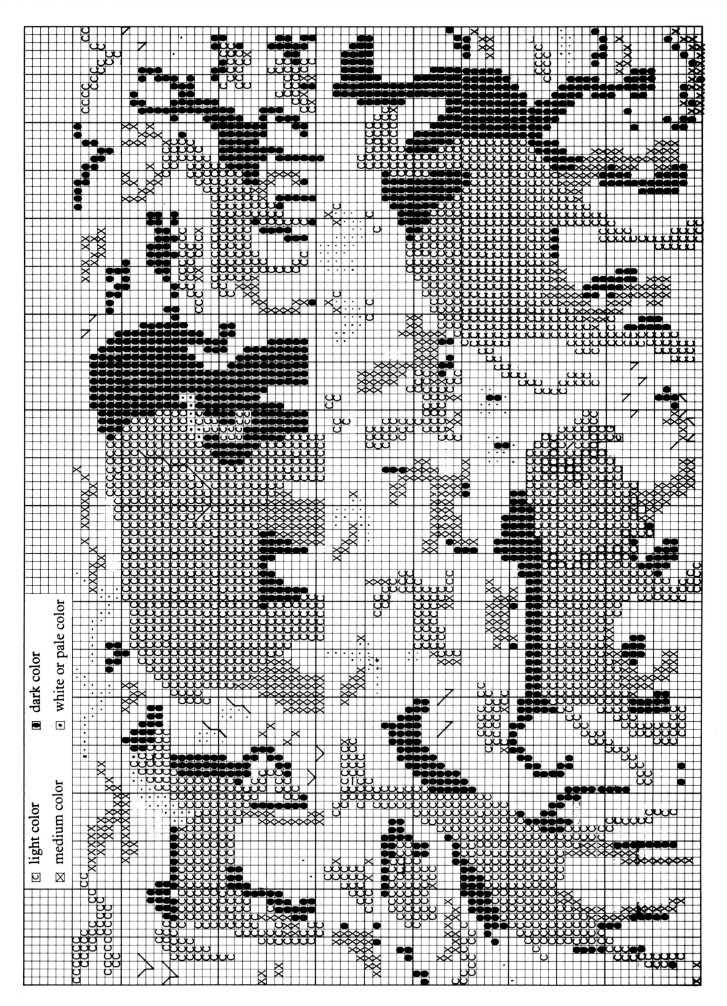

light color   dark color

medium color   white or pale color

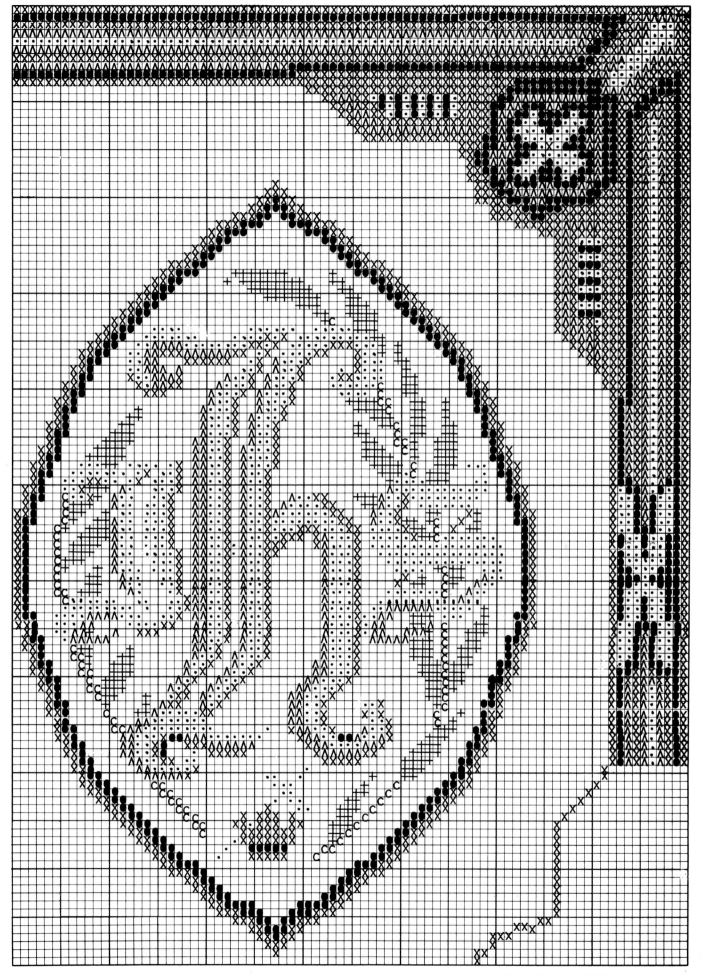

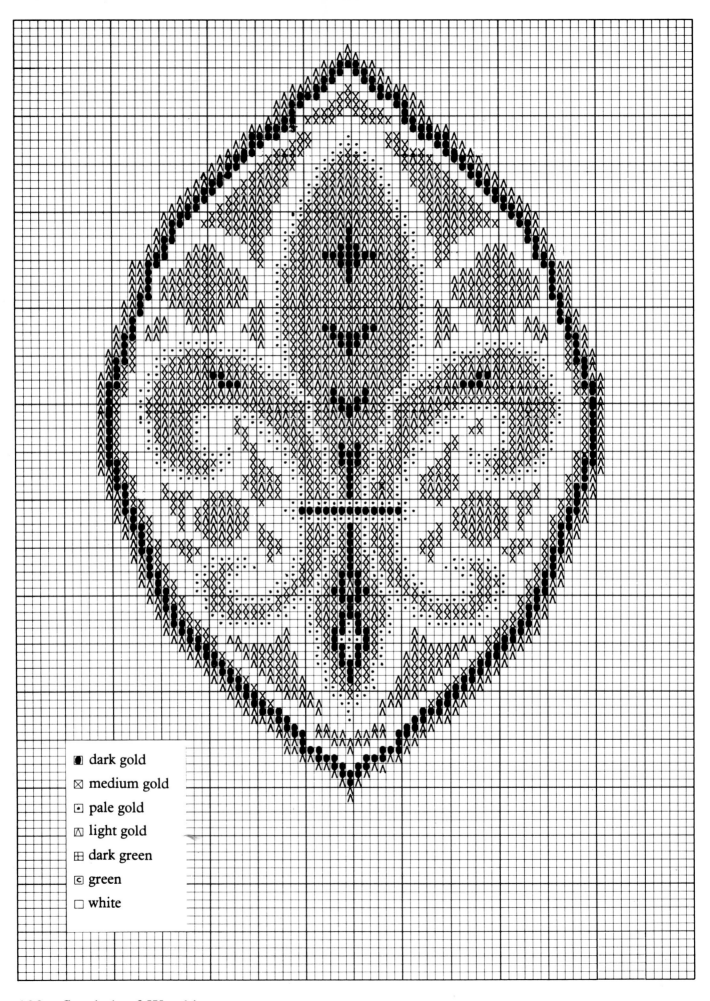

dark gold
medium gold
pale gold
light gold
dark green
green
white

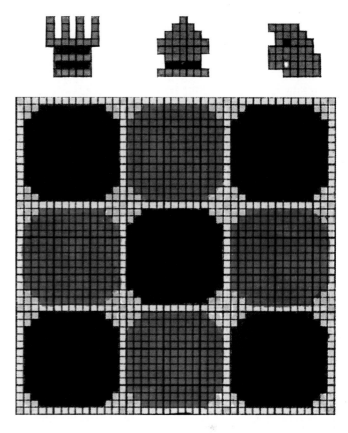

Fun & Games

■ —black   ◪ —blue

⊠ —red   ⊡ —yellow

▣ —grey   ⧅ —flesh

Bargello Backgammon Board

Turn the page upside-down and match edges as indicated in the diagram for the other half of the game board.

Work the entire board on bargello canvas in the following manner:

1. Work the points in the playing area of the board.

2. Work the background of the playing area from the center border down.

3. Work the two-stitch wide borders around the playing area with upright gobelin stitches. (See Stitch Dictionary in the Appendix.)

4. Work the decorative border in tent stitch.

Buttons in two contrasting colors make excellent playing pieces.

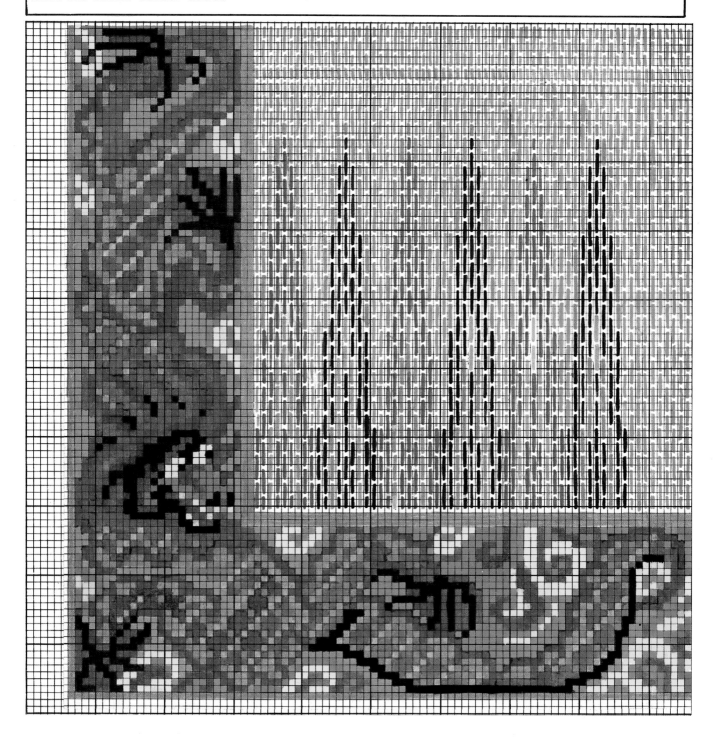

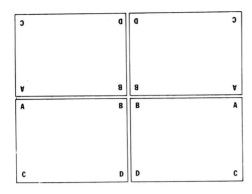

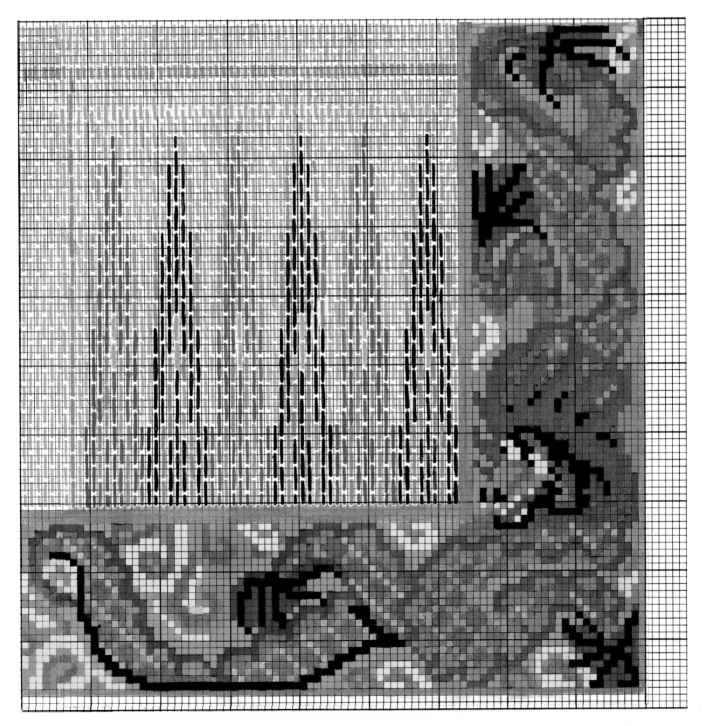

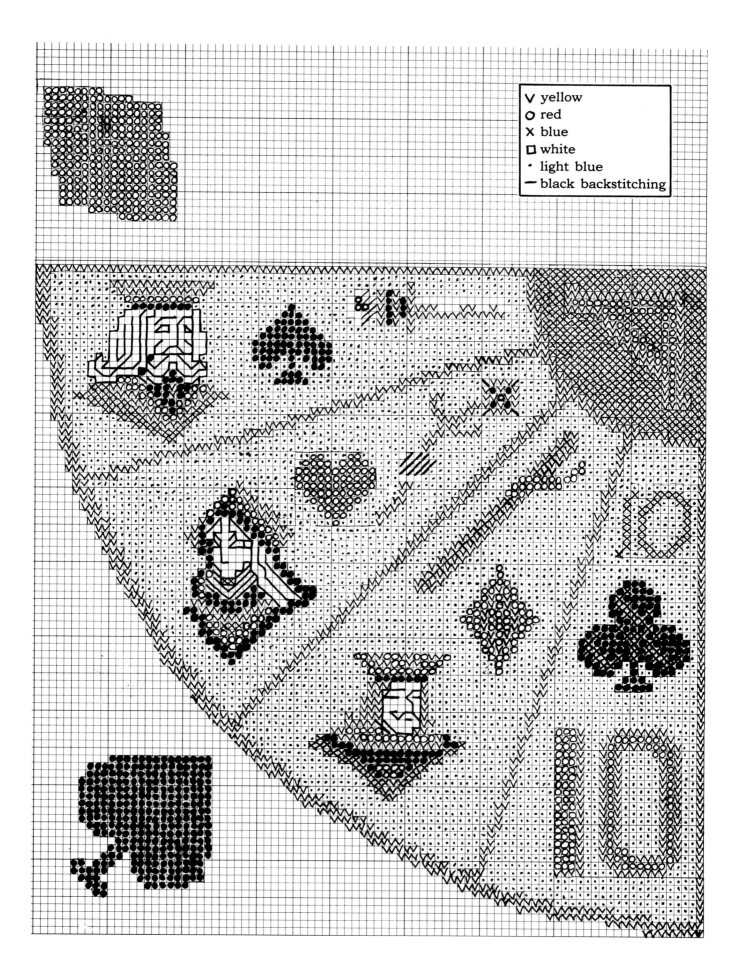

Dart Board

Work the dart board in needlepoint on plastic or interlocking mono canvas. (See Stitch Dictionary in the Appendix.) The background offers an excellent opportunity to work some of the decorative needlepoint stitches.

Since you will not want to tear your needlework with sharp darts, try covering ping pong balls with strips of velcro. These will stick to the needlework without damaging the yarn.

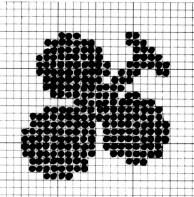

Turn the page upside-down and match edges for the other half of the pattern.

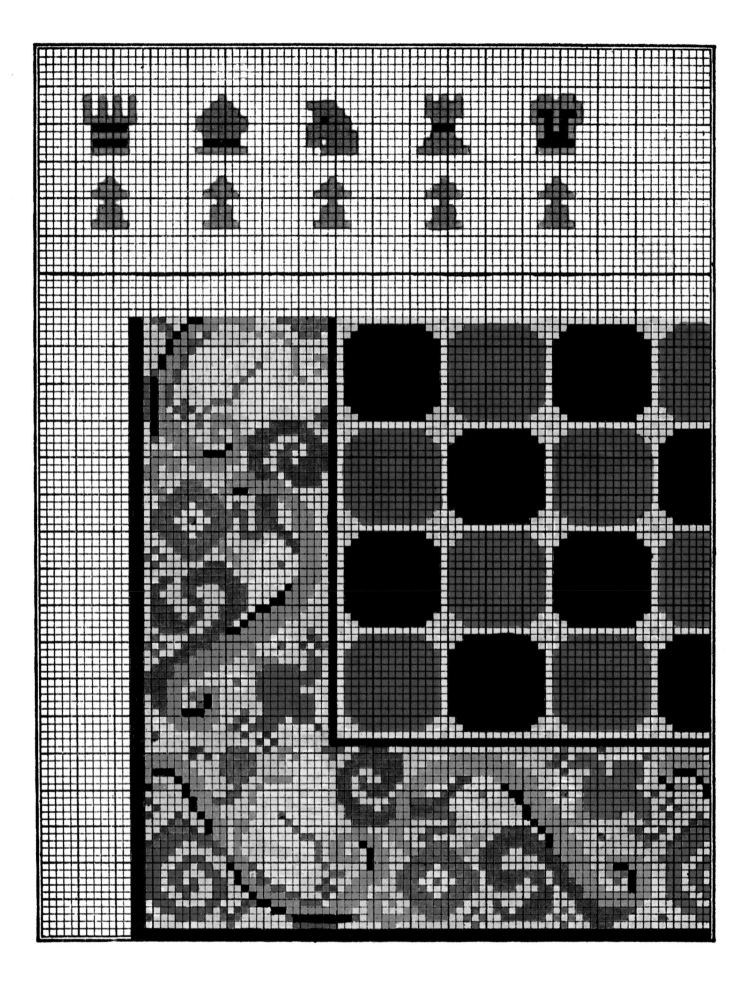

Chess/Checker Board

Turn the page upside down and match edges for the other half of the game board.

Work the entire board in basketweave on plastic or interlocking mono canvas. (See Stitch Dictionary in the Appendix.)

Large buttons in two contrasting colors work well as checkers.

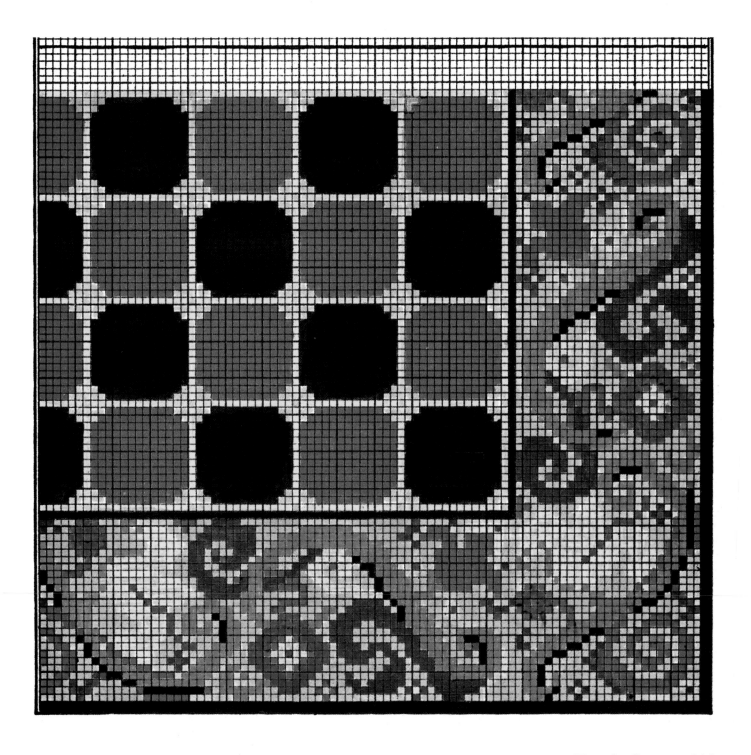

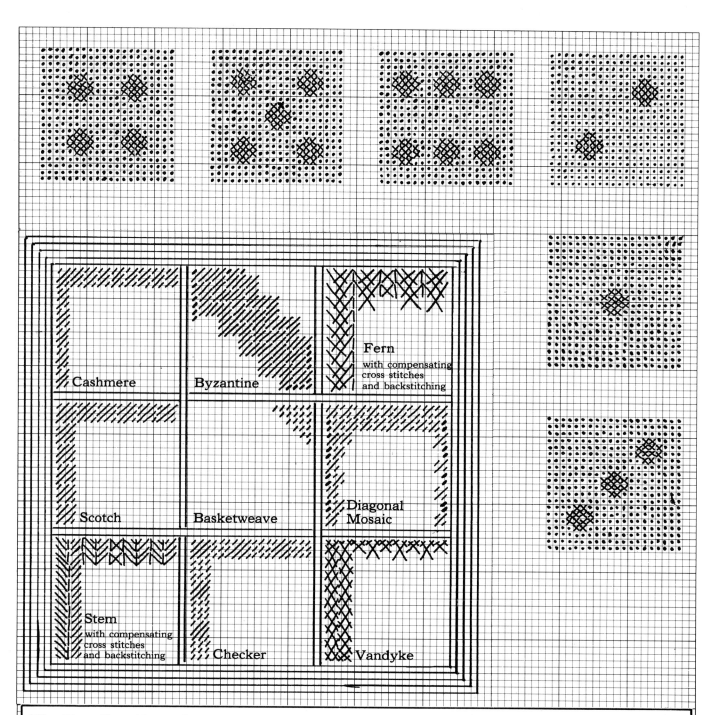

Tic-Tac-Toe Board

Work the entire game board on plastic or interlocking mono canvas.

Each square on the game board is worked in a different stitch. (See Stitch Dictionary in the Appendix for diagrams.) Anywhere that it is not possible to make a stitch the length shown in the stitch diagrams, make a compensating stitch. On the board diagram, some compensating stitches are shown by heavy black lines.

Work the border of the board in the following manner:

1 row of long-armed cross stitch covering two threads.

1 row of tent stitch covering one thread.

1 row of long-armed cross stitch covering two threads.

Work the inside borders around each square with 1 row of the long-armed cross stitch covering two threads.

Large buttons in two contrasting colors make excellent playing pieces.

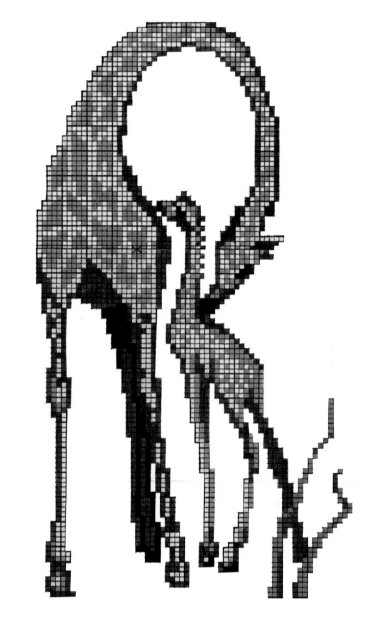

Animal Menagerie

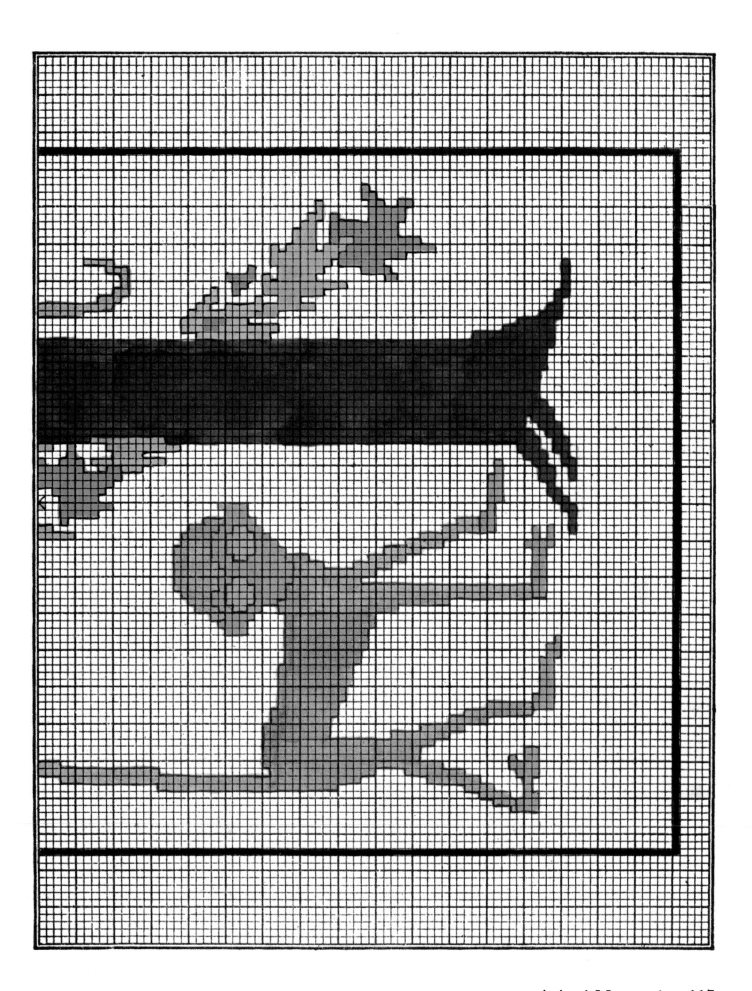

-black
-dark gray
-gray
-light gray
-green
-pink beige

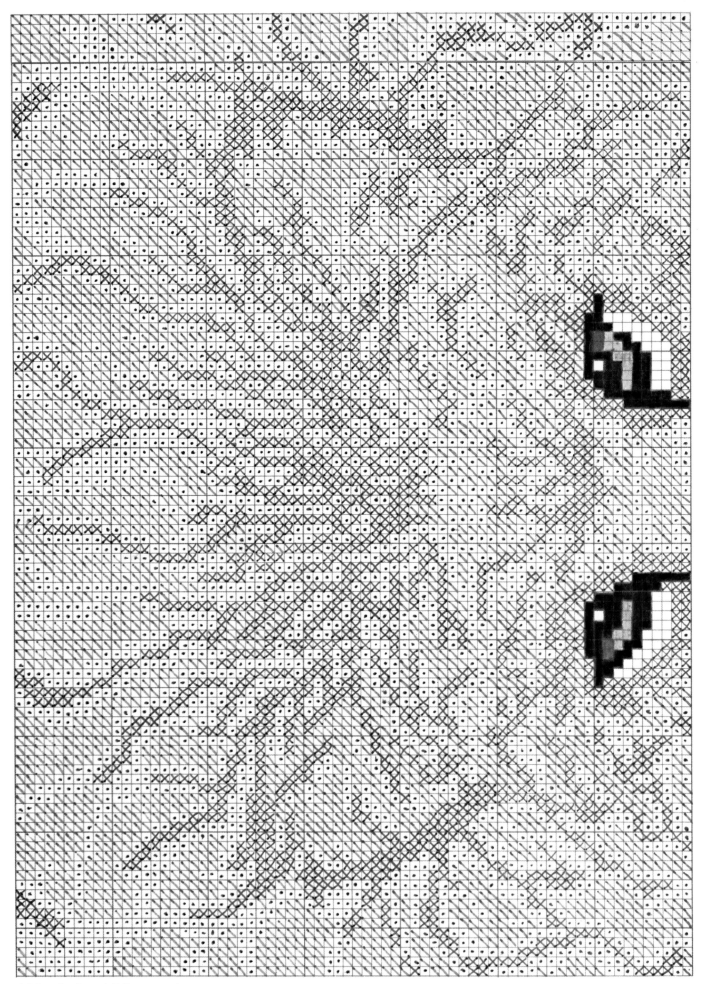

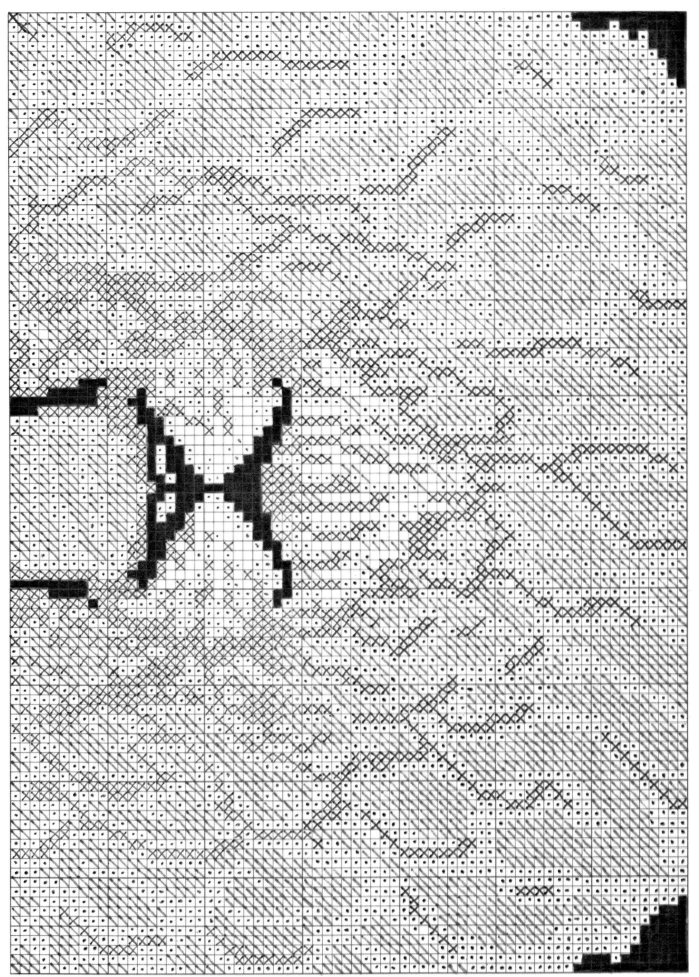

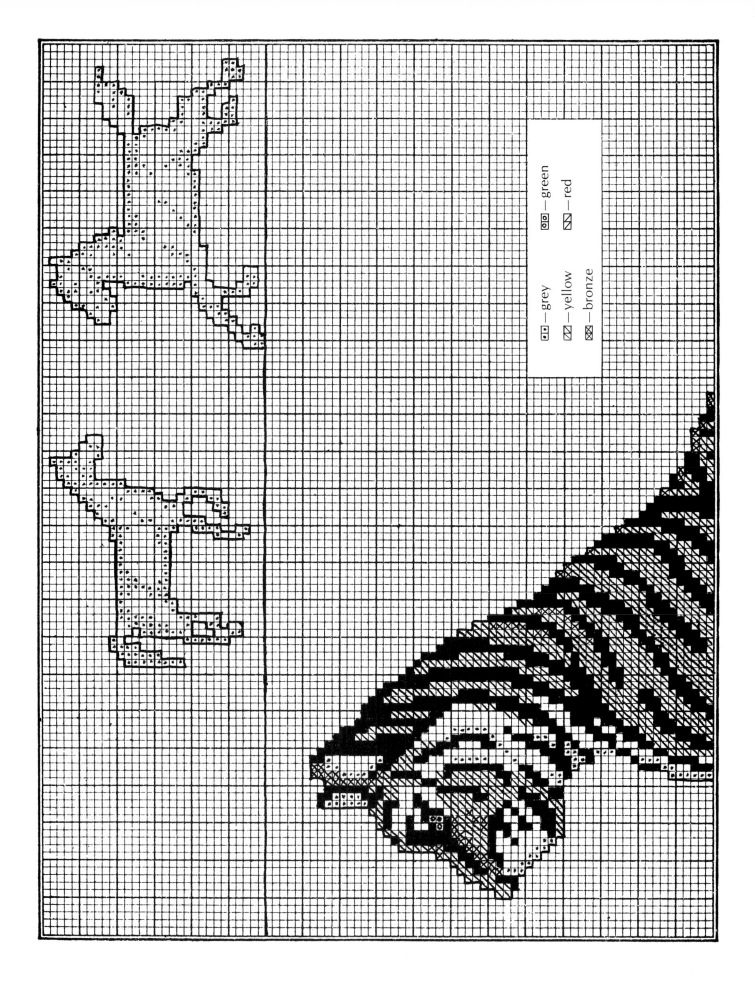

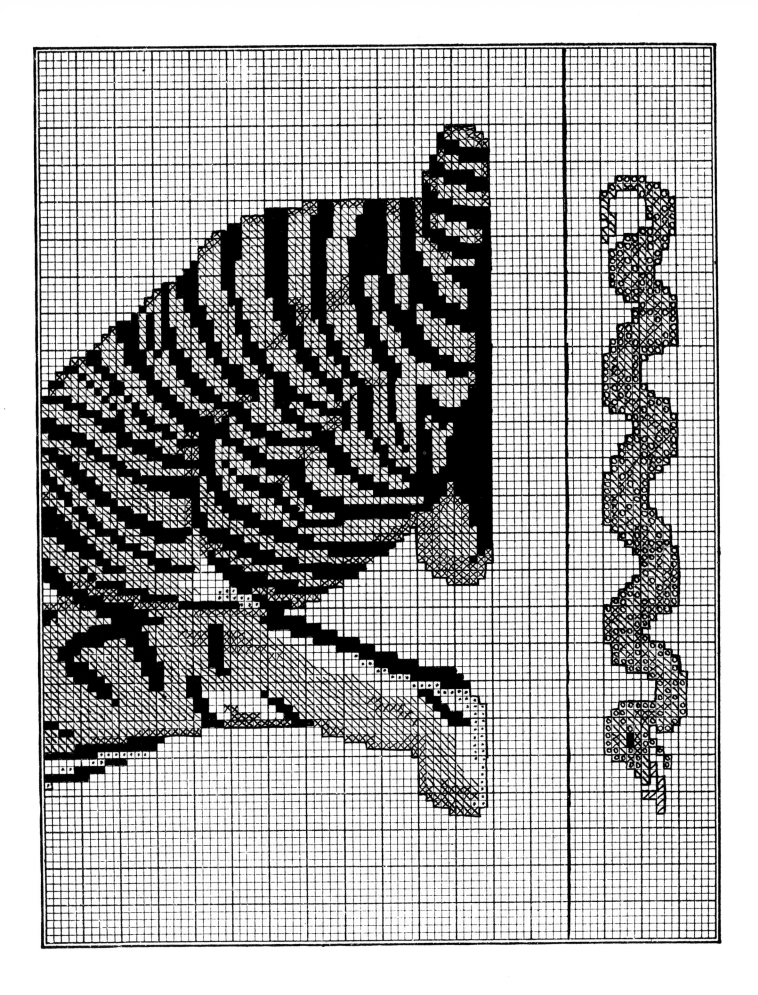

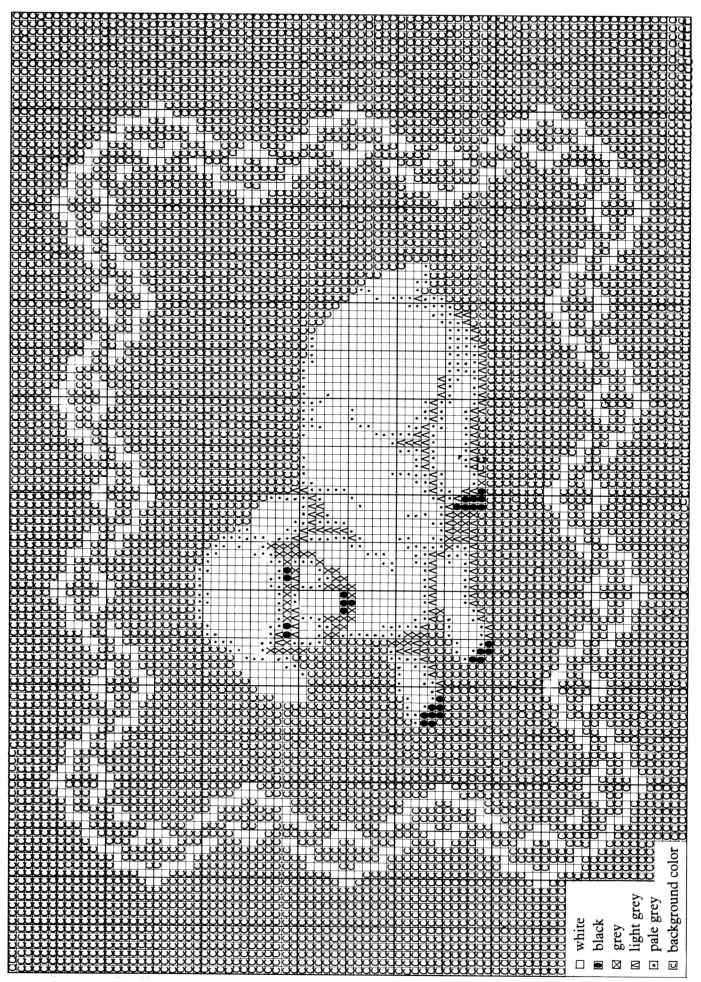

□ white
▣ black
⊠ grey
⊠ light grey
⊡ pale grey
☉ background color

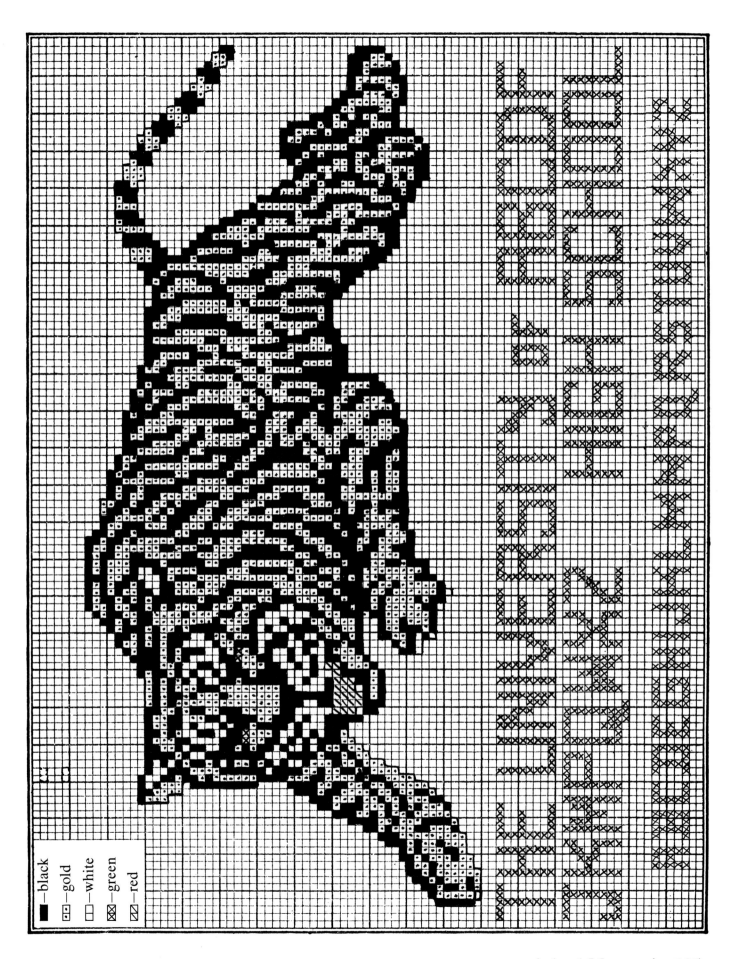

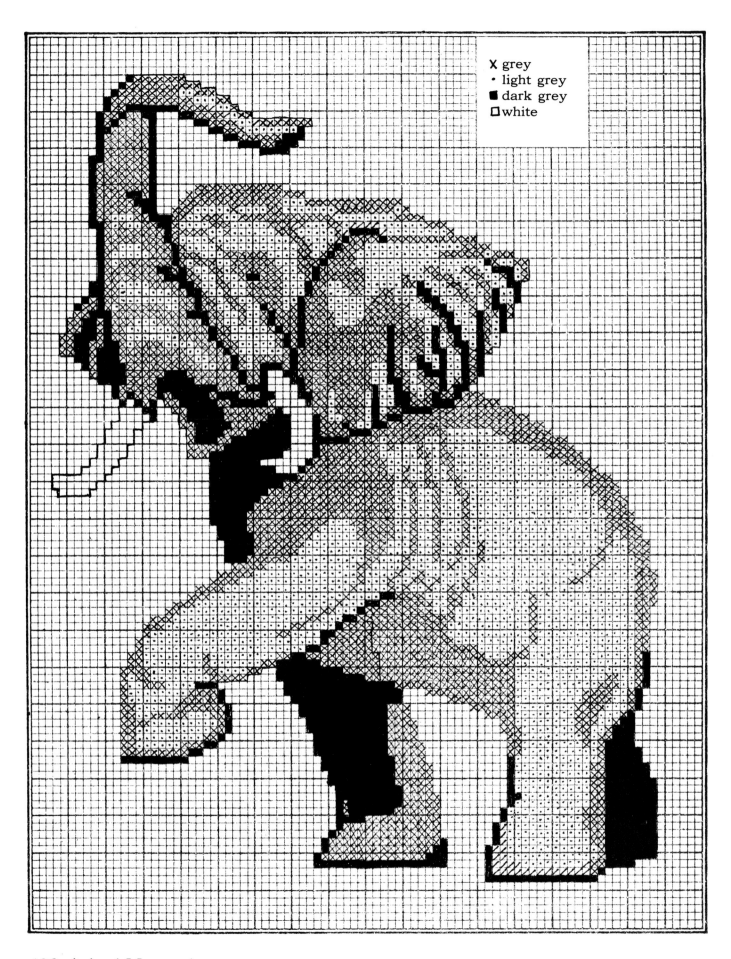

X grey
• light grey
■ dark grey
□ white

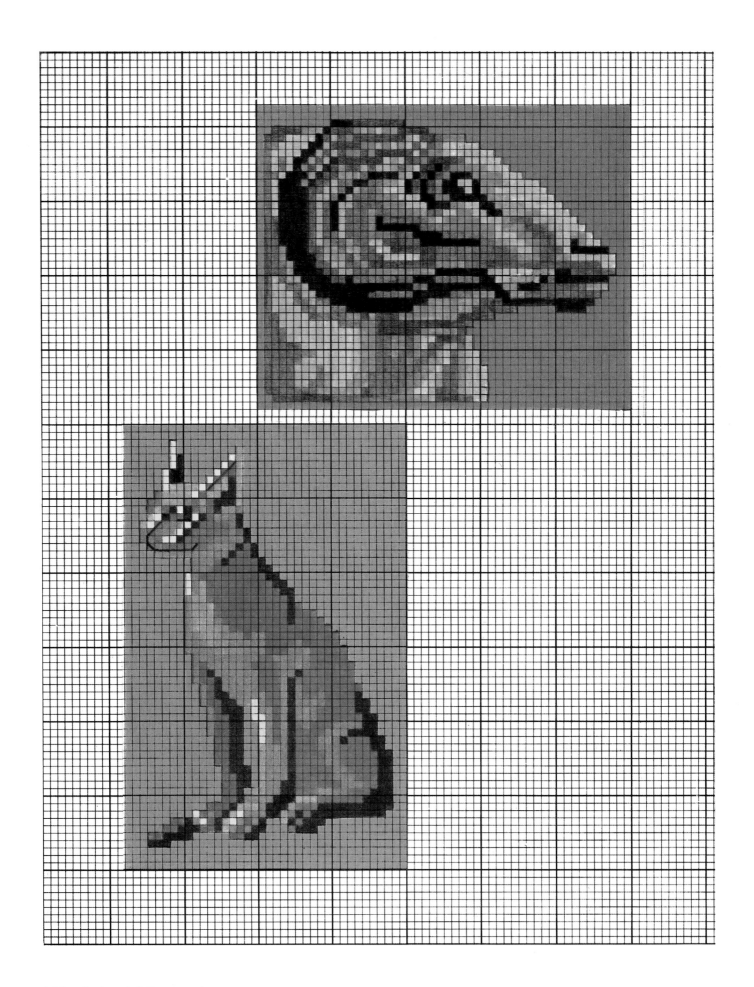

Around the World

130 Around the World

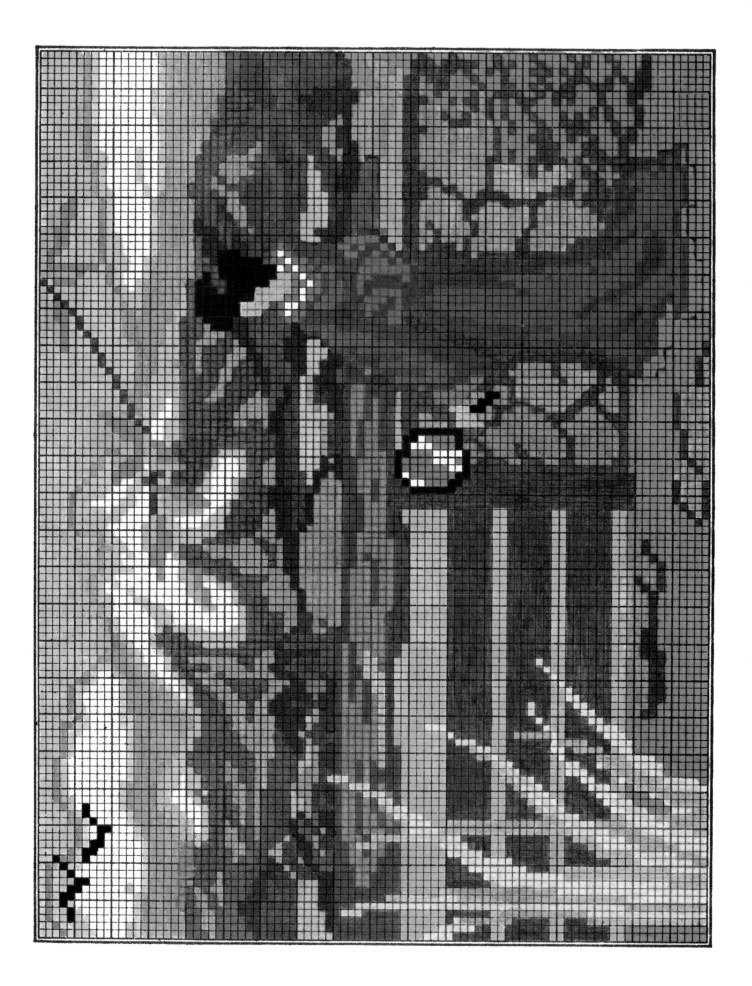

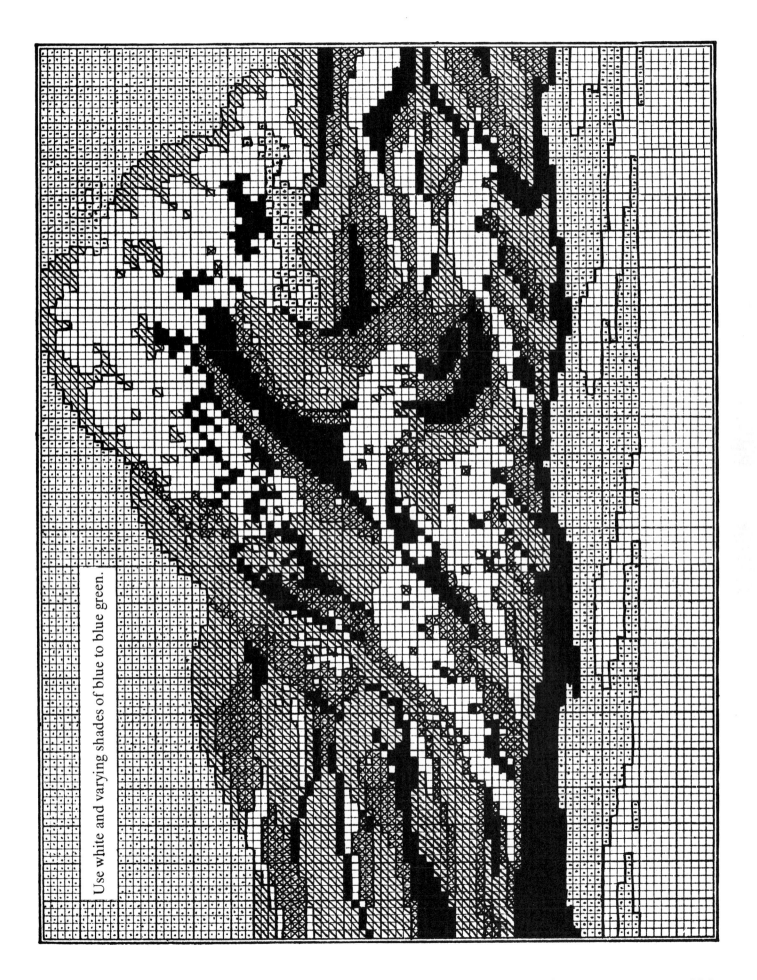

Use white and varying shades of blue to blue green.

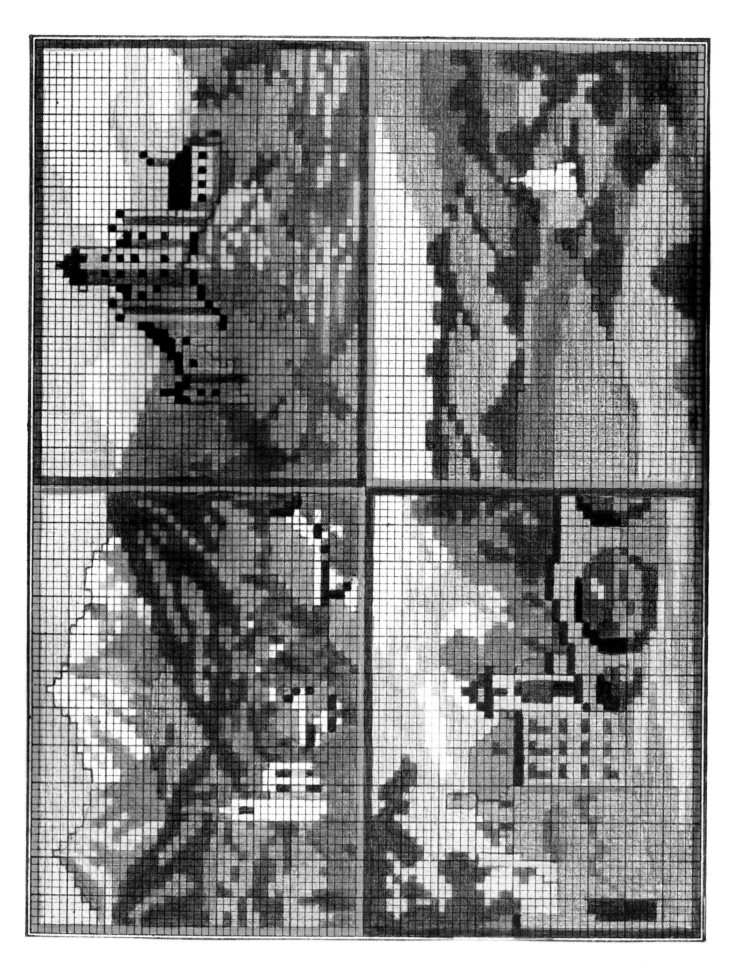

Use shades of a color such as ⊡ light beige through ⊠ beige, ⊠ light brown and ■ brown; or ⊡ pale gray, ⊠ gray, ⊠ charcoal, and ■ black; or shades of blue or of gold. Shades of two different colors may also be combined in one design.

⊡⊡ —white
⊠⊠ —green
⊙⊙ —red

The upper right hand corner shows a diagram for working in Bargello. Each stitch covers 4 canvas threads, except where compensating. It will be easier to work with the canvas turned sideways in order that the left side becomes the top and the stitches are worked vertically. Stitches marked —— should be worked in white.

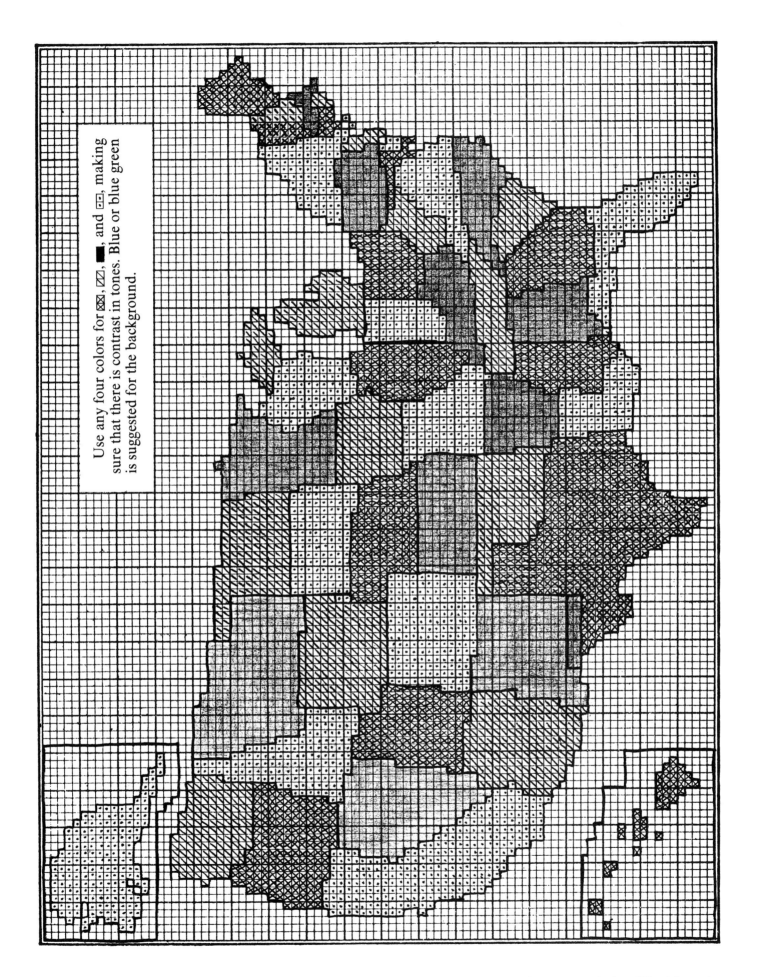

Use any four colors for ⊠, ⧄, ■, and ⊡, making sure that there is contrast in tones. Blue or blue green is suggested for the background.

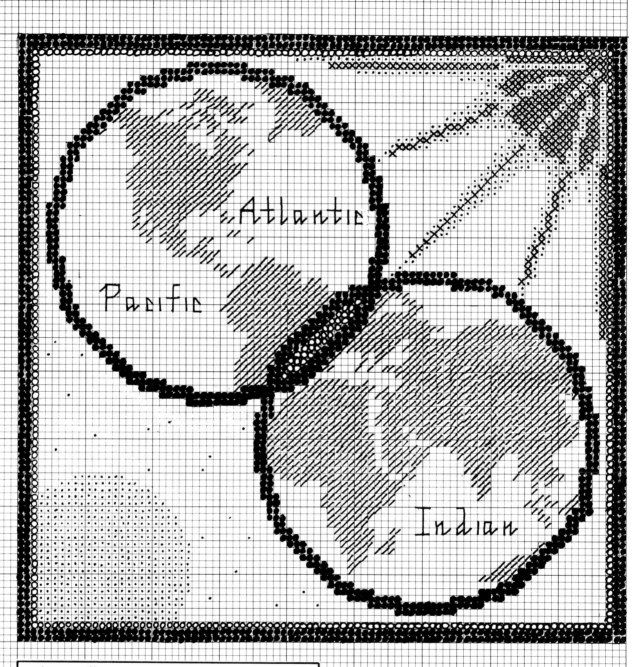

x deep yellow
· pale yellow
● brown
○ gold brown
/ green

background—light blue inside circles
blue outside circles
backstitching—brown for names of oceans

Serendipity

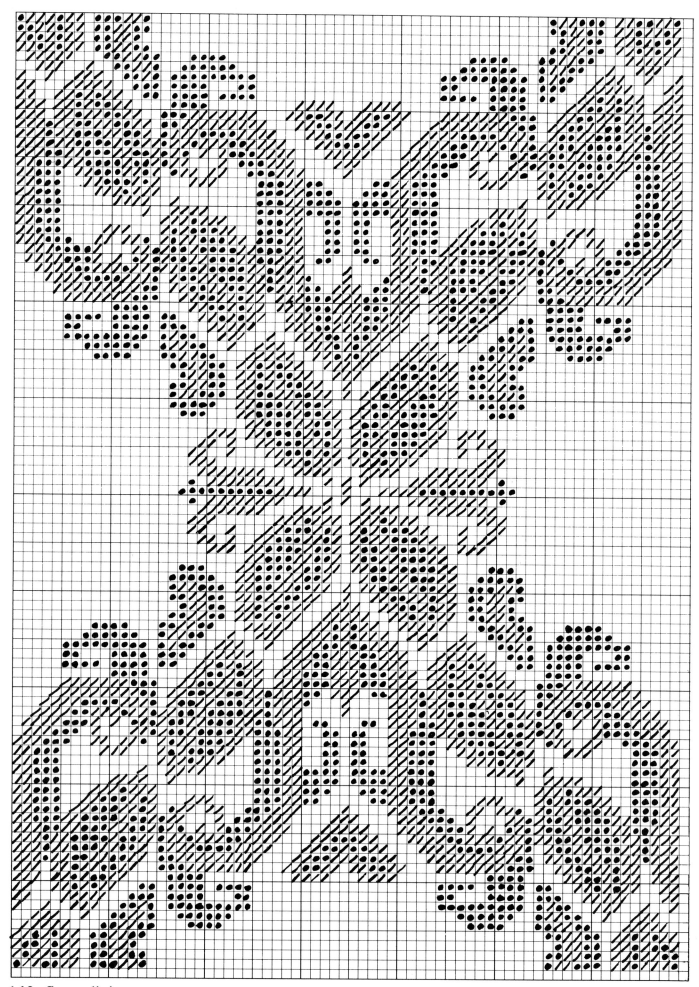

142 Serendipity

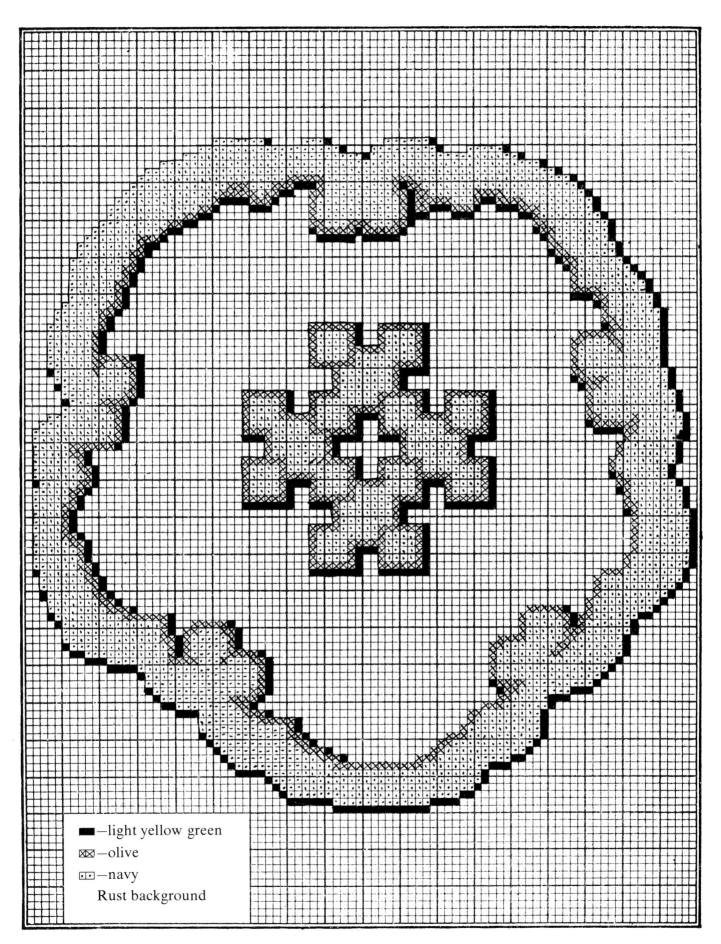

■ —light yellow green

⊠ —olive

▫ —navy

Rust background

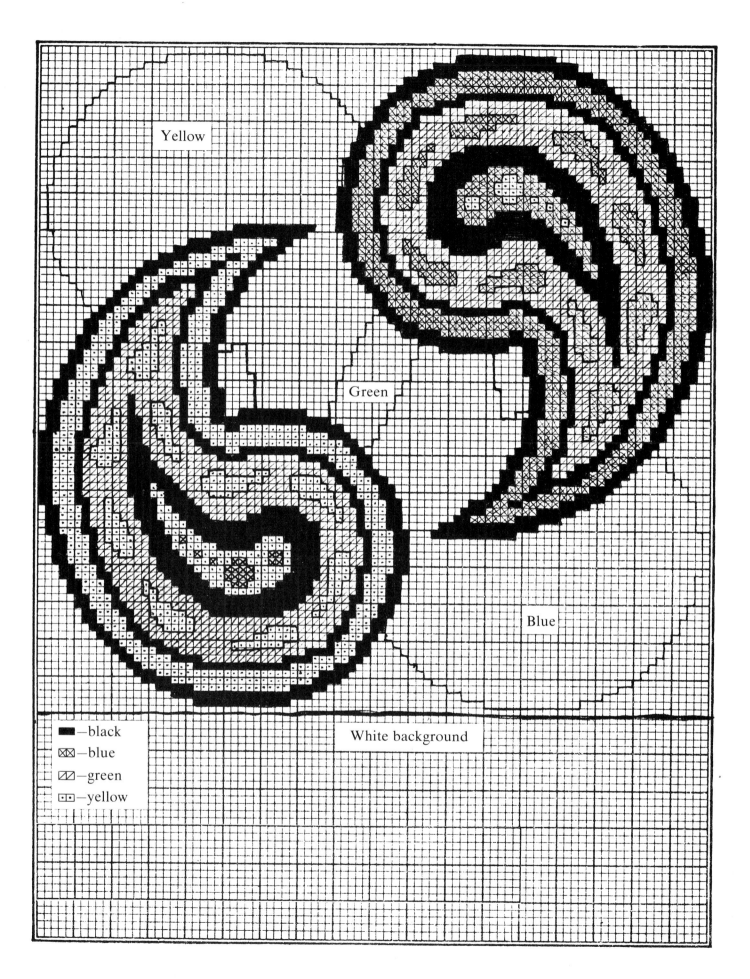

Yellow

Green

Blue

White background

■ —black
⊠ —blue
▨ —green
⊡ —yellow

144 Serendipity

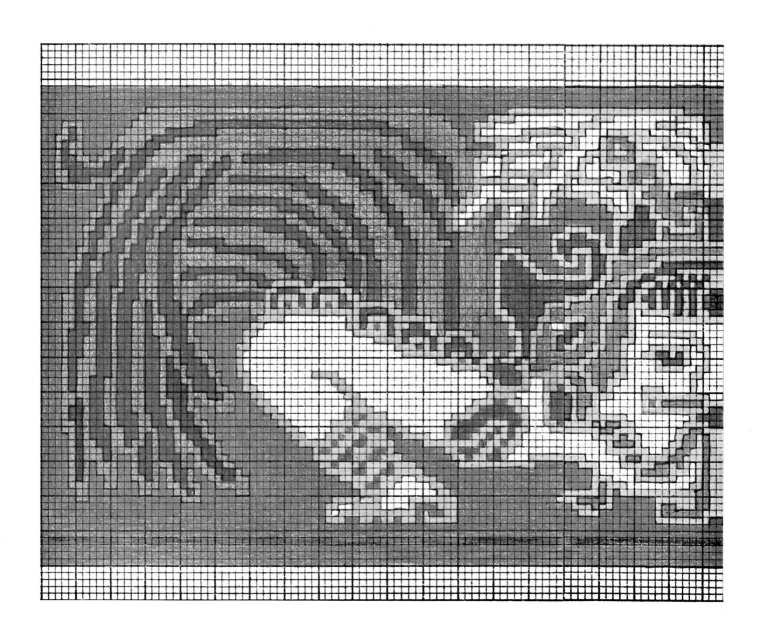

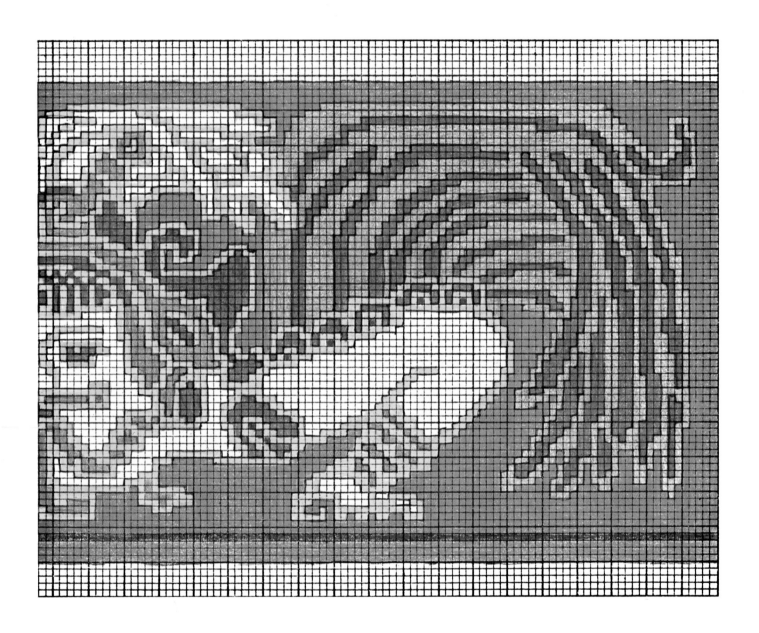

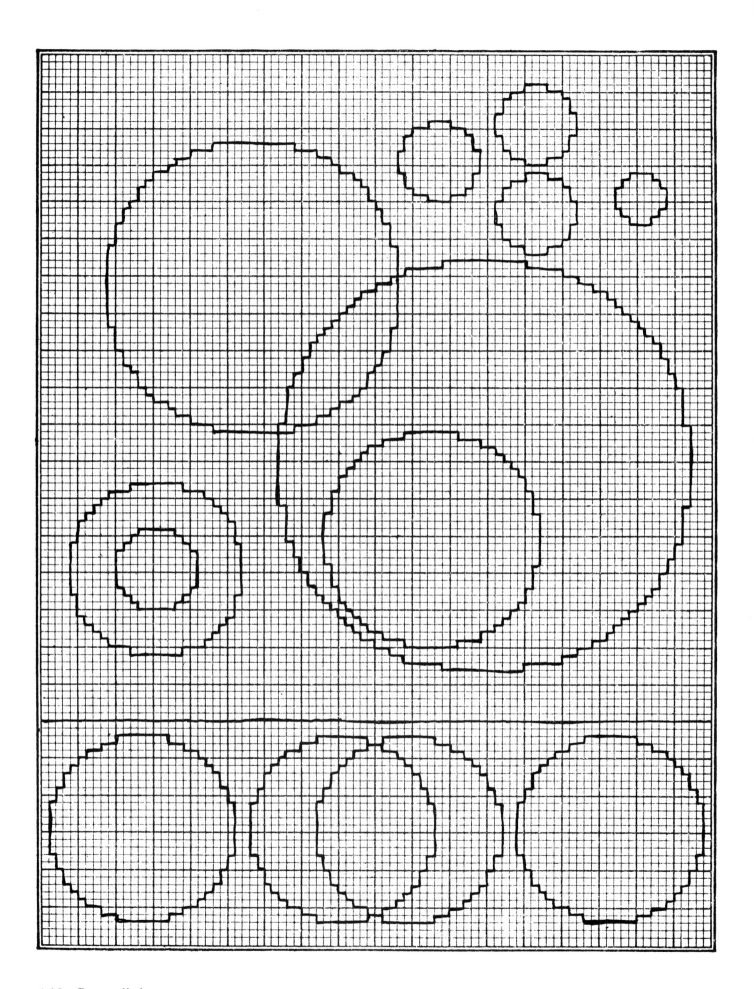

148 Serendipity

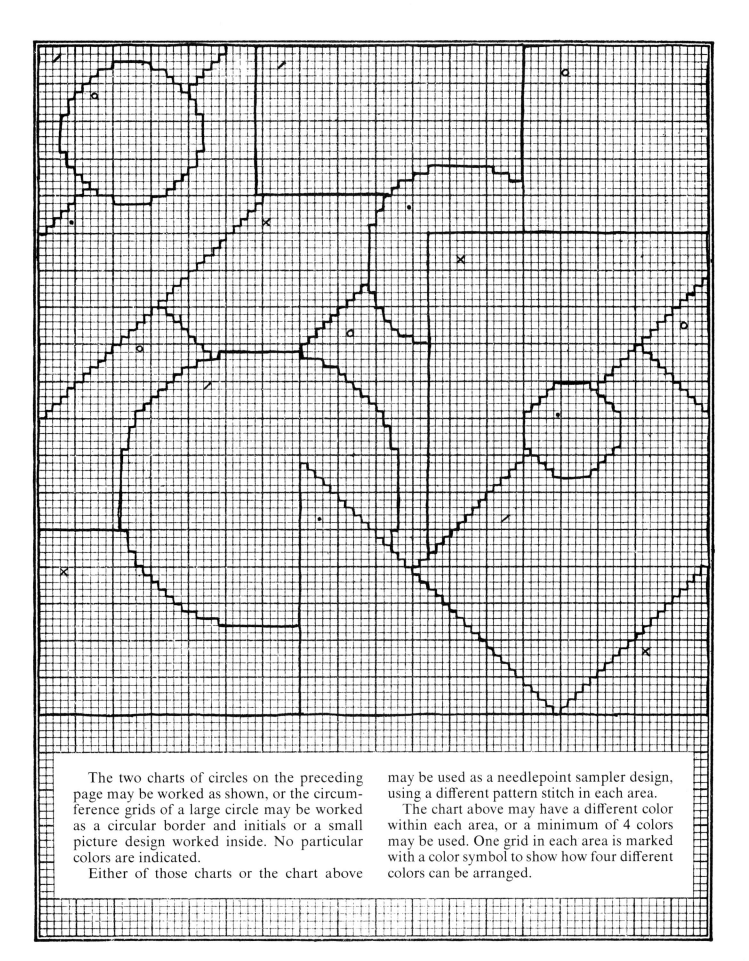

The two charts of circles on the preceding page may be worked as shown, or the circumference grids of a large circle may be worked as a circular border and initials or a small picture design worked inside. No particular colors are indicated.

Either of those charts or the chart above

may be used as a needlepoint sampler design, using a different pattern stitch in each area.

The chart above may have a different color within each area, or a minimum of 4 colors may be used. One grid in each area is marked with a color symbol to show how four different colors can be arranged.

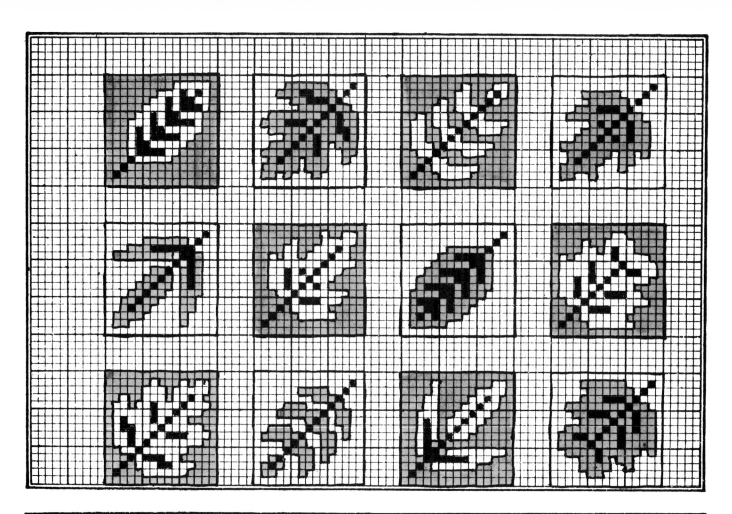

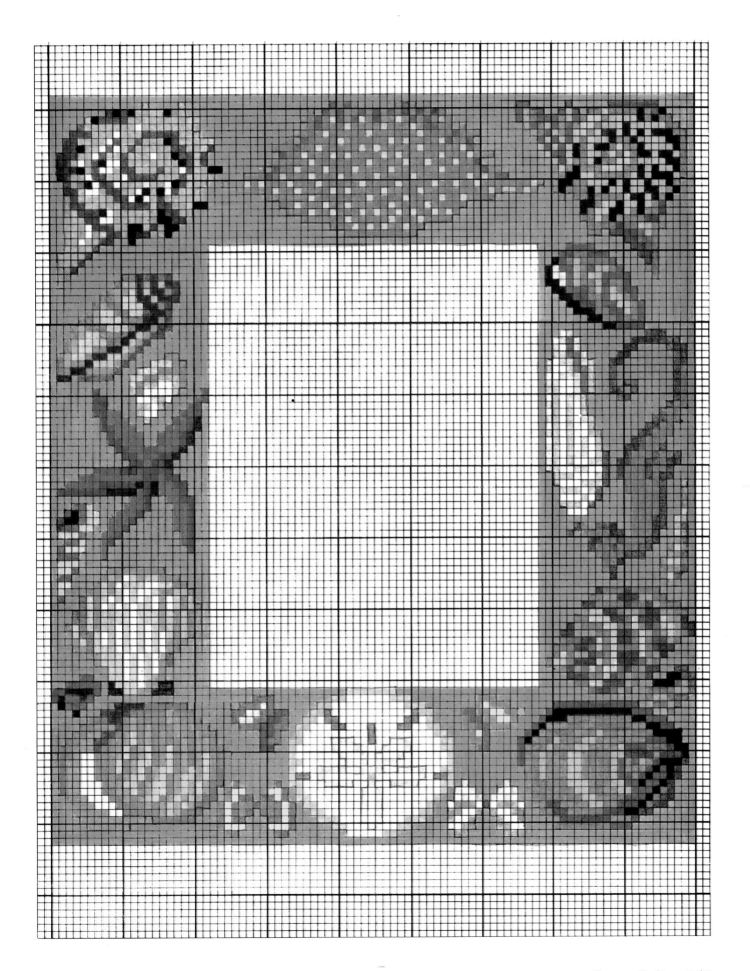

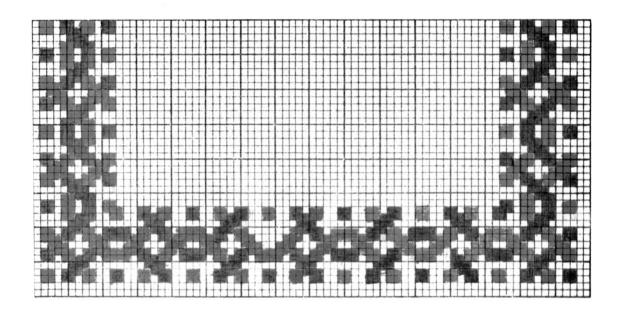

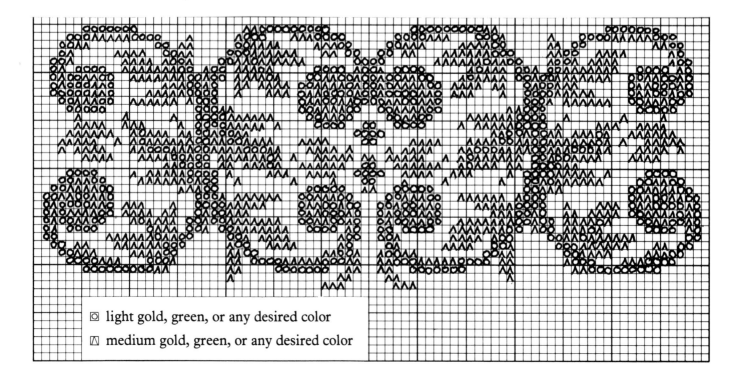

◙ light gold, green, or any desired color

⩑ medium gold, green, or any desired color

motto

Family name

Use colors to correspond to your family's coat of arms.

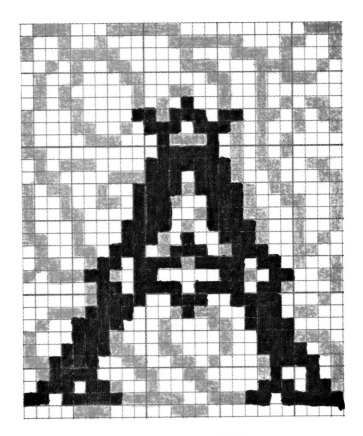

A to Z

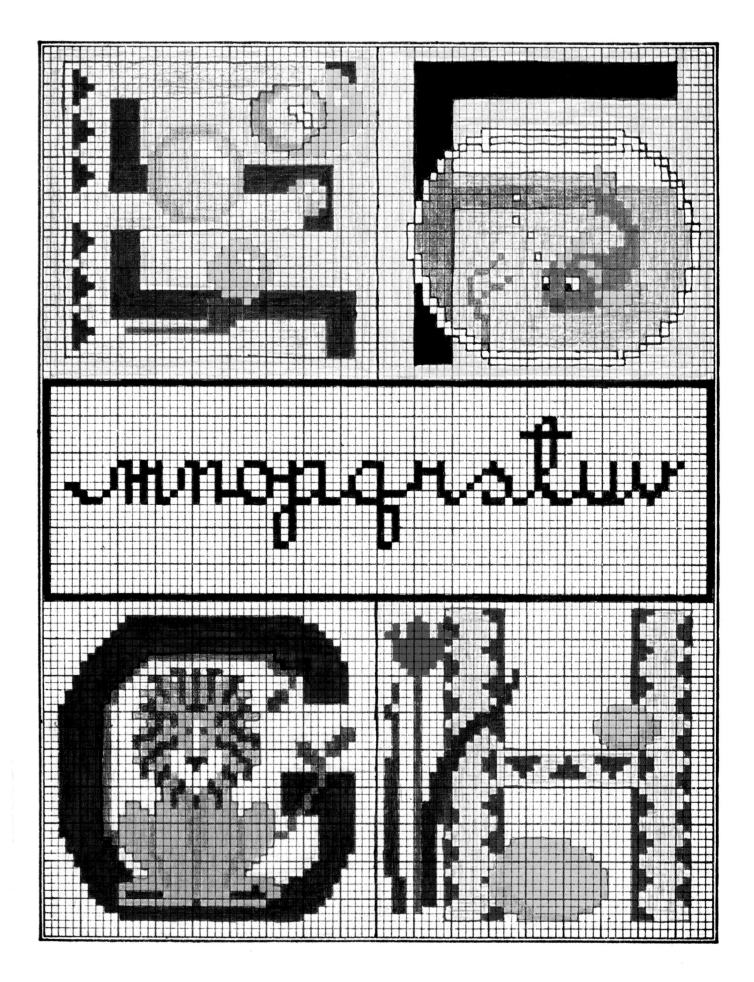

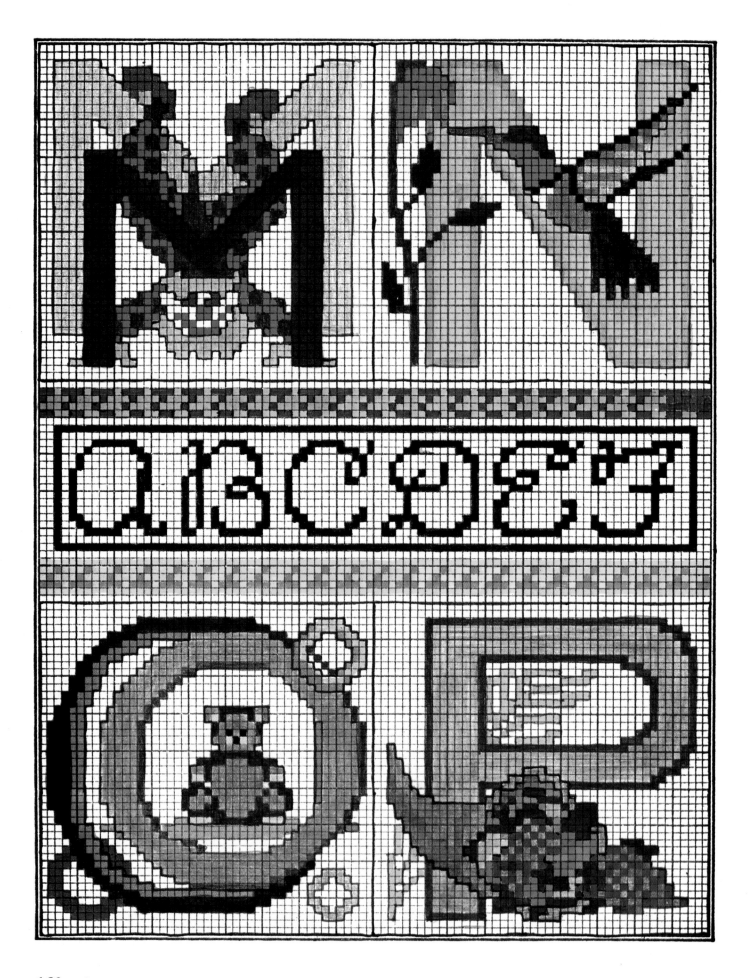

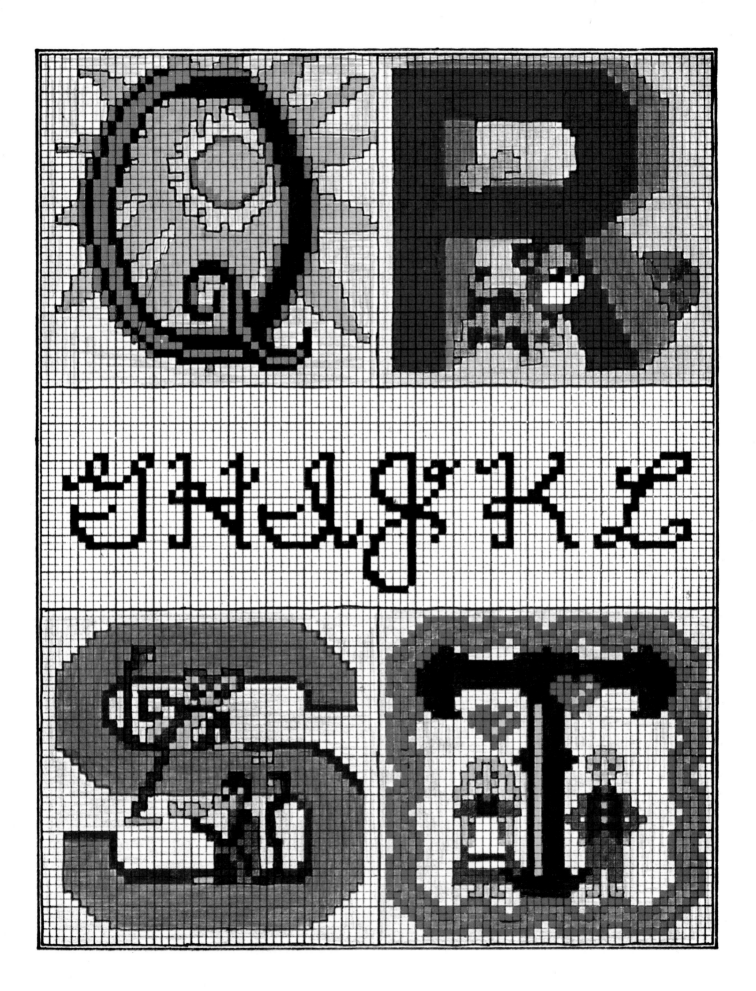

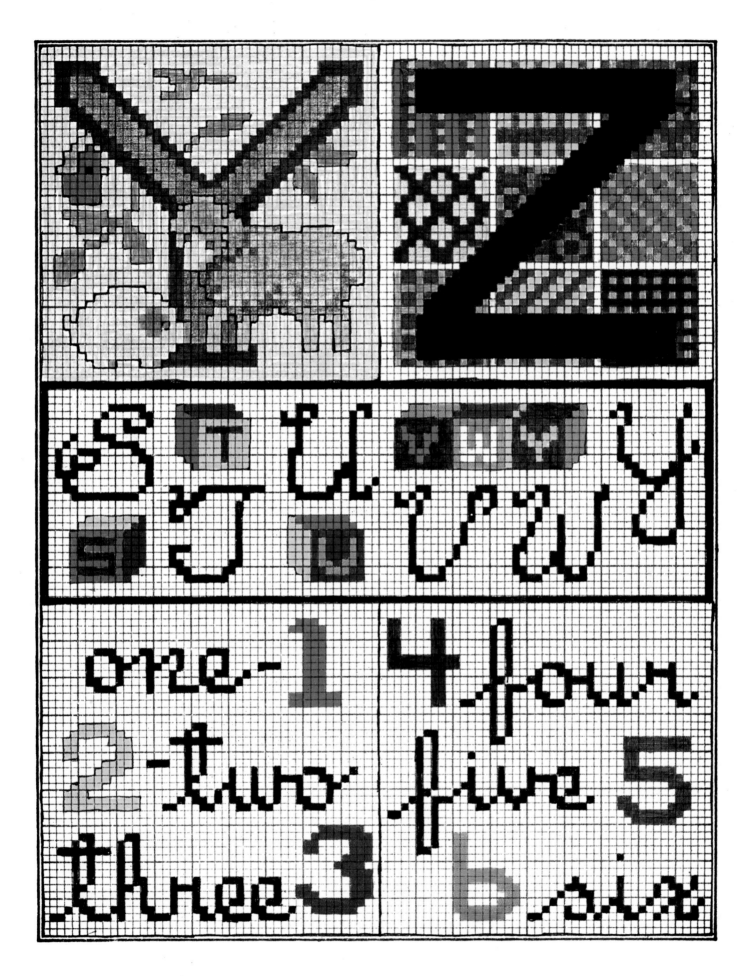

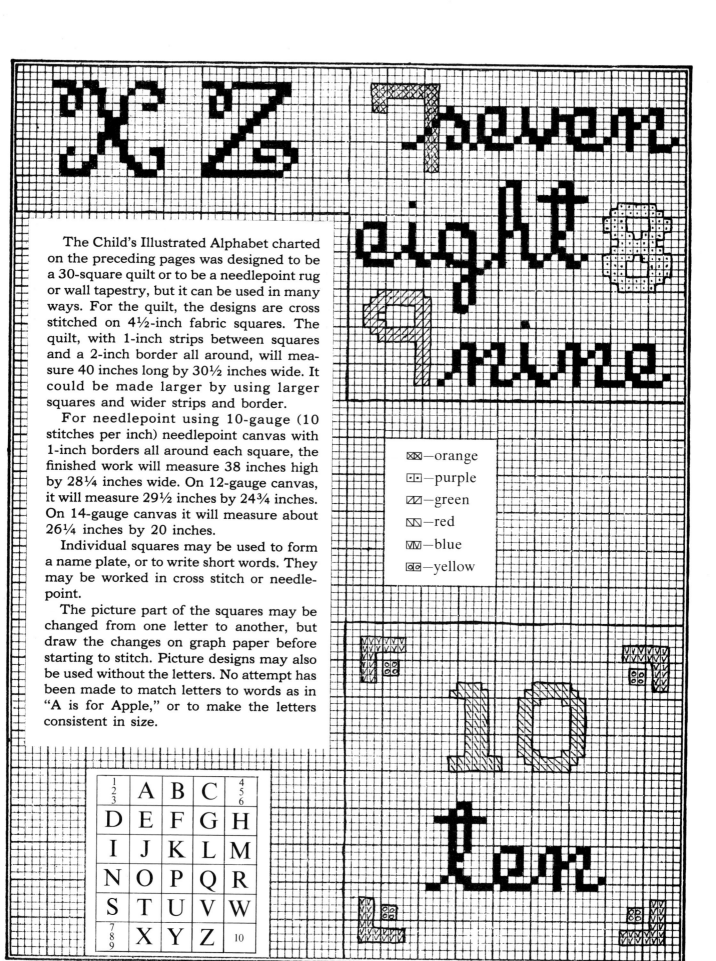

The Child's Illustrated Alphabet charted on the preceding pages was designed to be a 30-square quilt or to be a needlepoint rug or wall tapestry, but it can be used in many ways. For the quilt, the designs are cross stitched on 4½-inch fabric squares. The quilt, with 1-inch strips between squares and a 2-inch border all around, will measure 40 inches long by 30½ inches wide. It could be made larger by using larger squares and wider strips and border.

For needlepoint using 10-gauge (10 stitches per inch) needlepoint canvas with 1-inch borders all around each square, the finished work will measure 38 inches high by 28¼ inches wide. On 12-gauge canvas, it will measure 29½ inches by 24¾ inches. On 14-gauge canvas it will measure about 26¼ inches by 20 inches.

Individual squares may be used to form a name plate, or to write short words. They may be worked in cross stitch or needle-point.

The picture part of the squares may be changed from one letter to another, but draw the changes on graph paper before starting to stitch. Picture designs may also be used without the letters. No attempt has been made to match letters to words as in "A is for Apple," or to make the letters consistent in size.

⊠⊠—orange
⊡⊡—purple
⬚⬚—green
⬚⬚—red
⬚⬚—blue
⬚⬚—yellow

1 2 3	A	B	C	4 5 6
D	E	F	G	H
I	J	K	L	M
N	O	P	Q	R
S	T	U	V	W
7 8 9	X	Y	Z	10

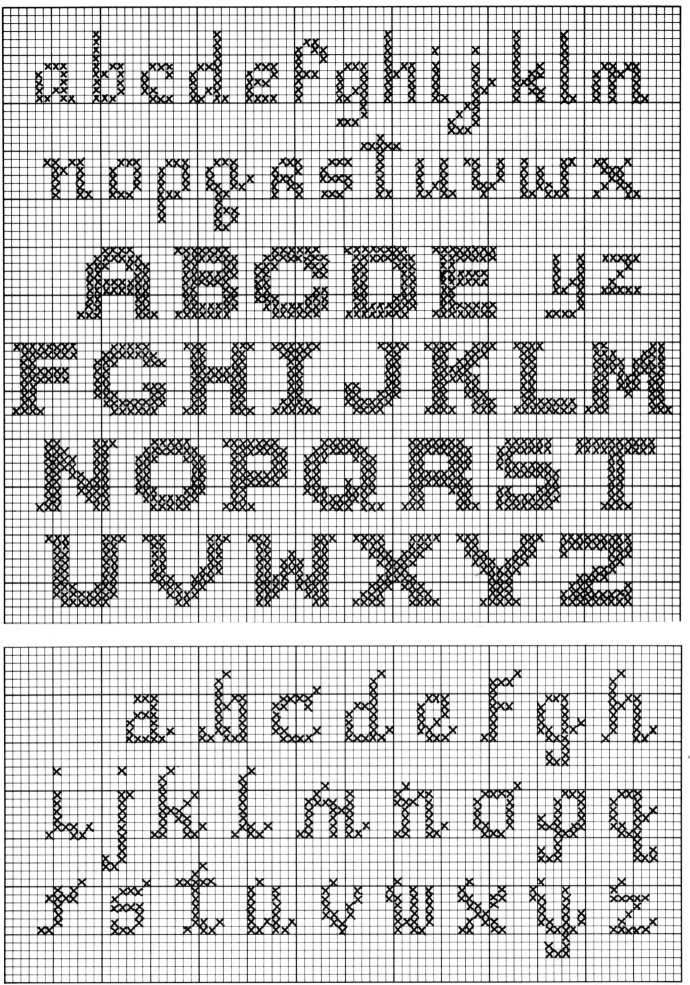

abcdefghijklm
nopqrstuvwx
y
z

ABCDE yz
FGHIJKLM
NOPQRST
UVWXYZ

abcdefgh
ijklmnopq
rstuvwxyz

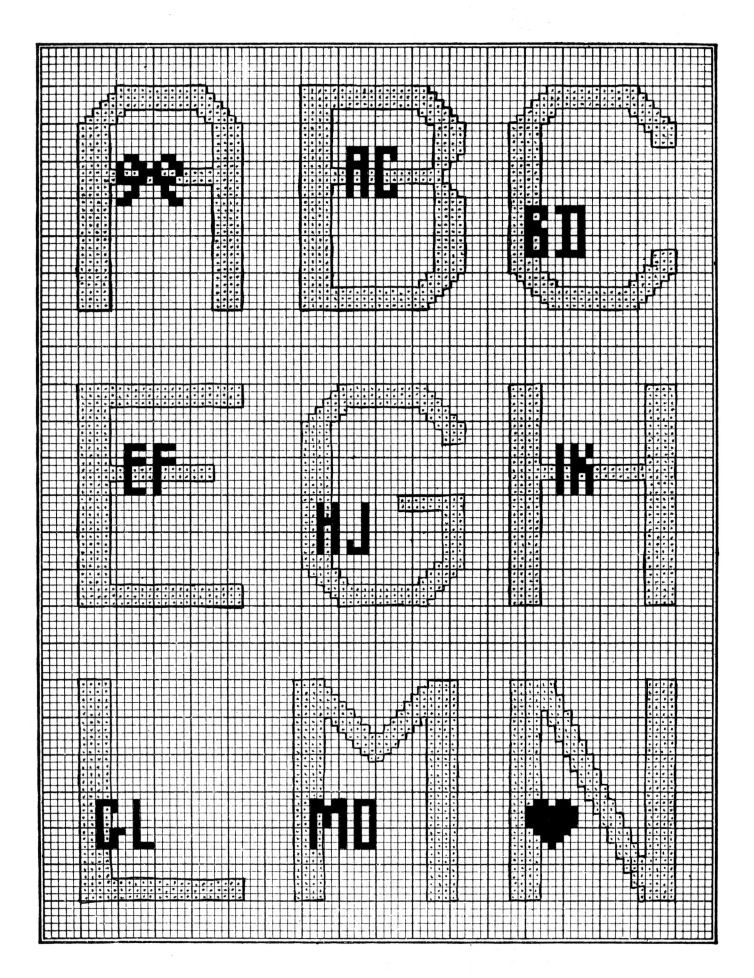

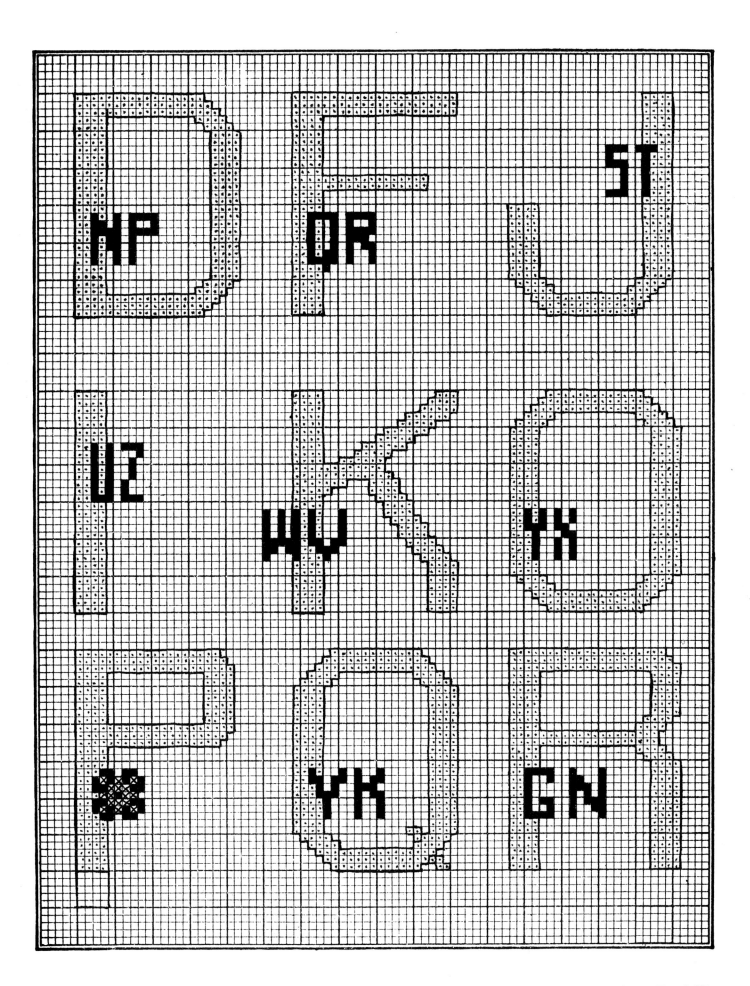

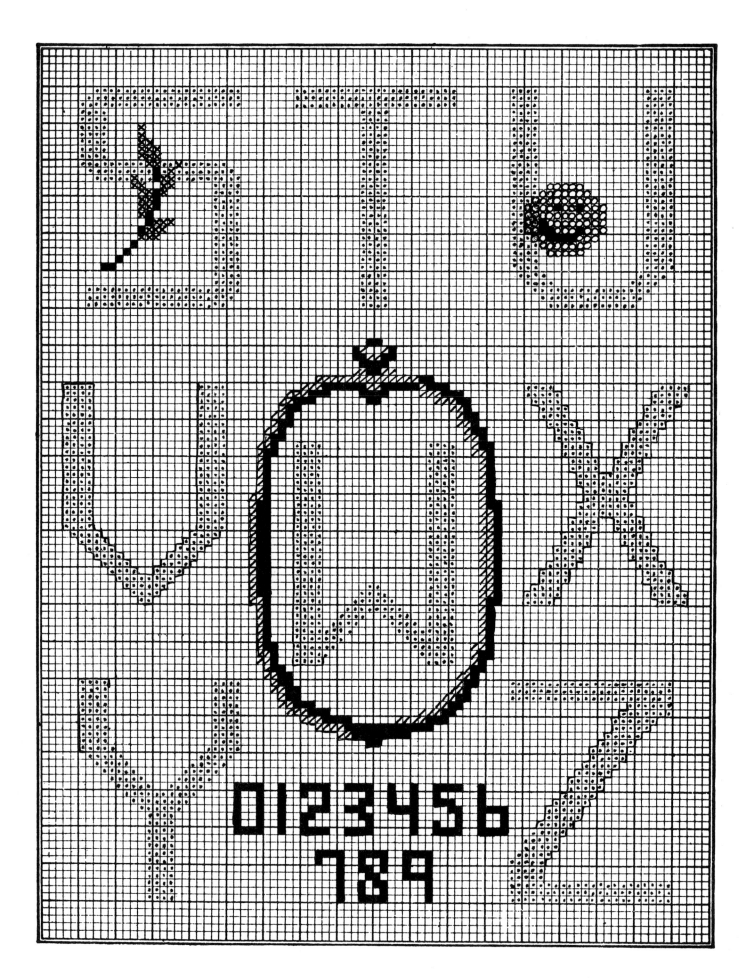

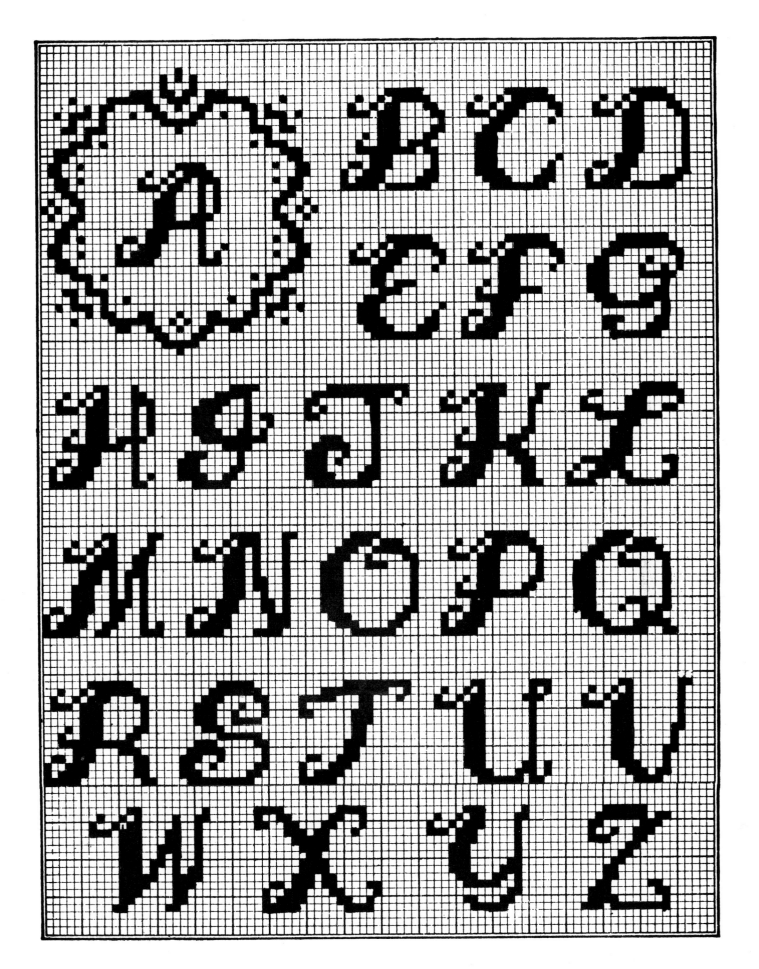

Before the invention of the printing press, books had to be copied by hand. This was a long and laborious process, and it gave rise to a guild of specialists in lettering. These specialists refined their skills to such a point that they created the beautifully intricate illuminated letters which are often associated with Bibles. The lettering of the older manuscripts became as much of an art form as was the actual text that was copied. Illuminated letters evoke almost automatically a religious connotation, even today.

The alphabet that follows can be used in one of two ways. The letters may be stitched alone, or you may stitch them over one of the illuminated backgrounds as illustrated here with the letters I, H, S, and Z. Stitch the background completely first, then embroider the desired letter over it. Notice that each letter contains at least one little cross. The letter A appears on this chapter's divider page.

One suggestion for how these illuminated letters may be used is to choose a favorite Bible verse and stitch the first letter with the illuminated capital.

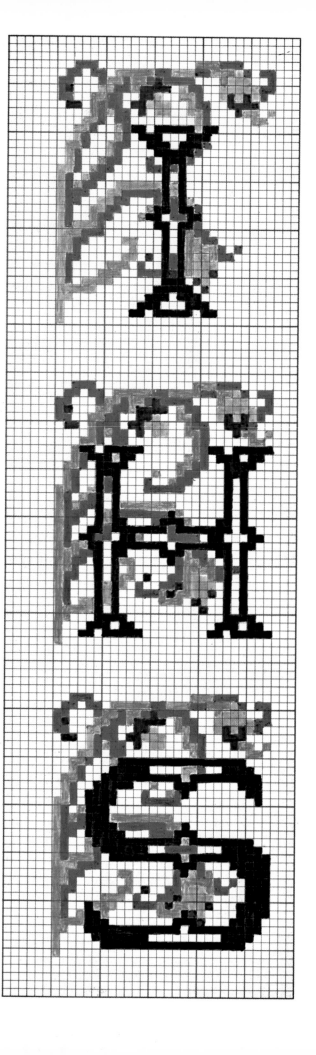

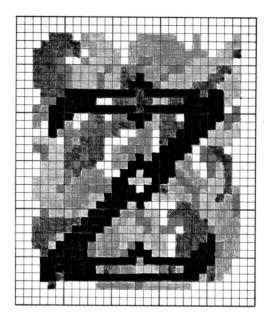

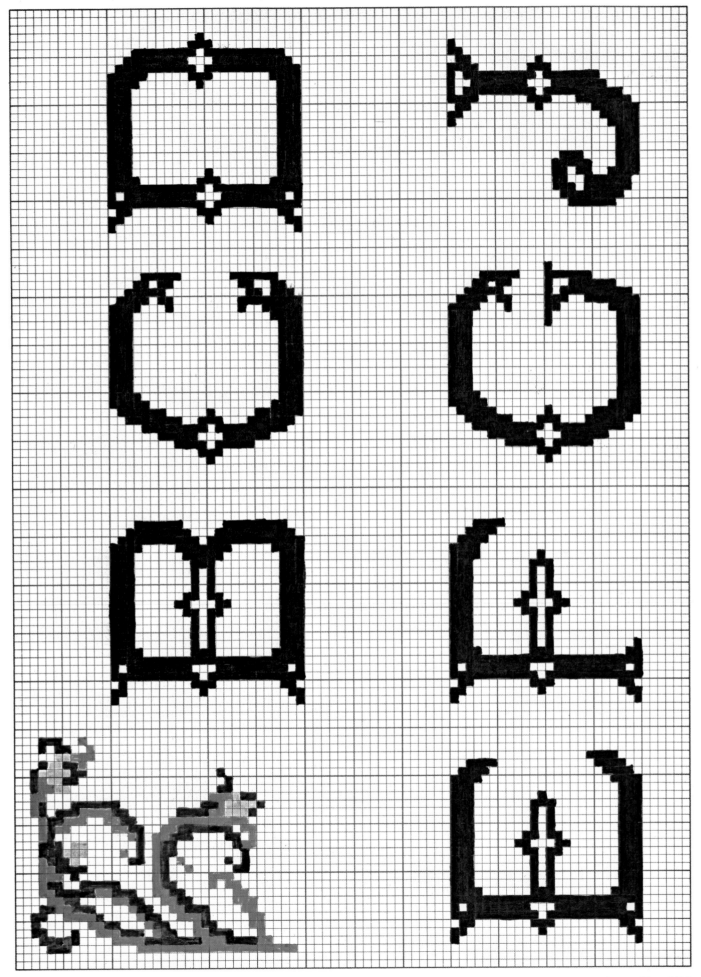

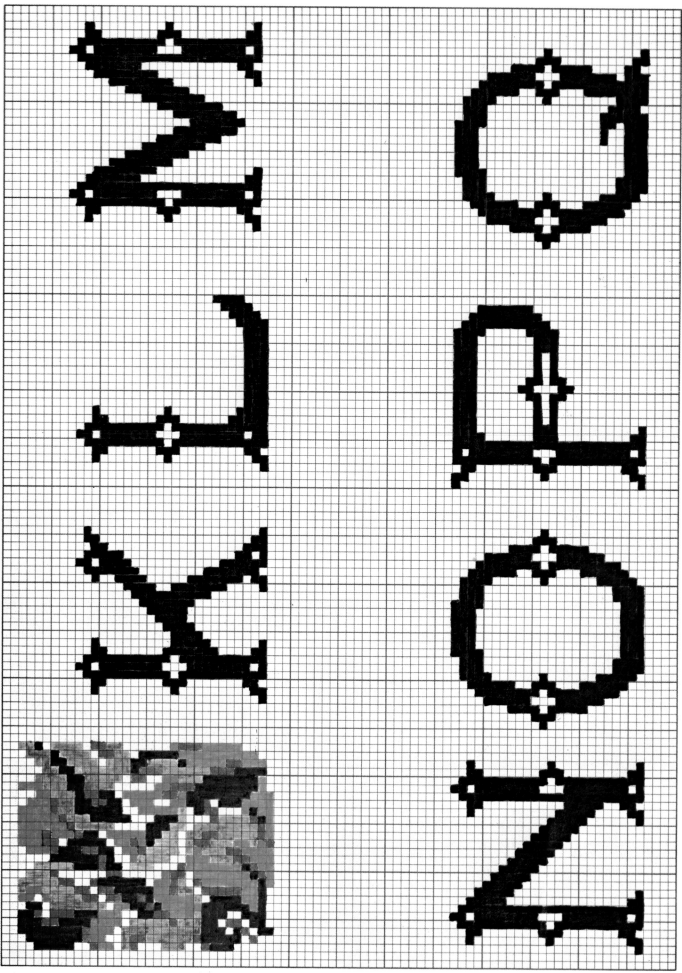

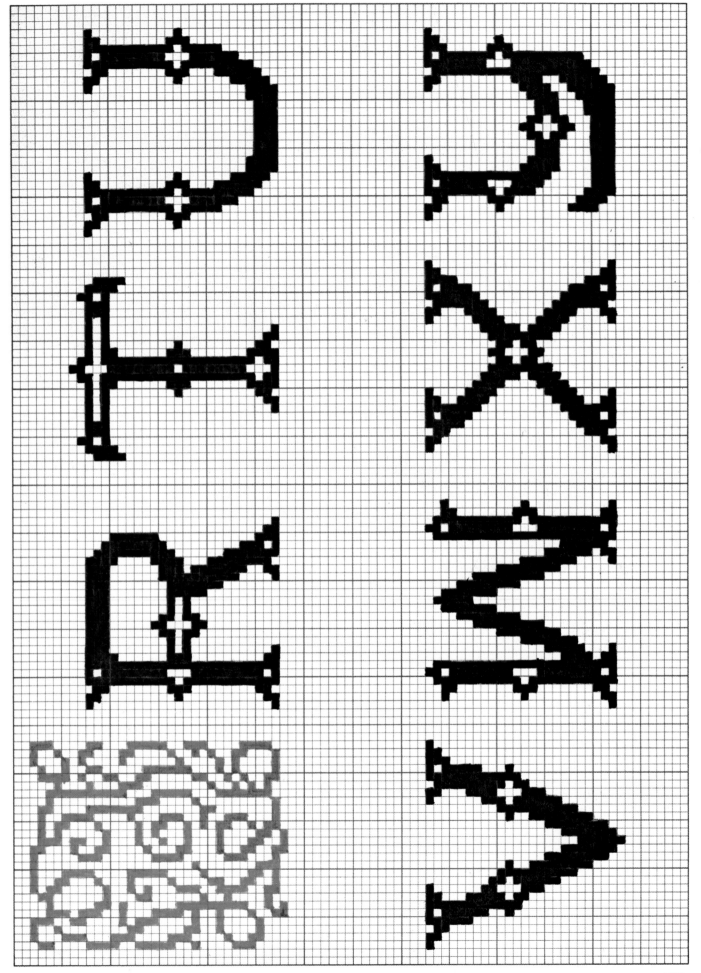

"When St. Peter announces "It's time to go" I'll say, PLEASE, LET ME FINISH, JUST— ONE——MORE——ROW—!!"

backstitching: glasses—gold metallic
yarn—light blue

174

Appendix

Working from a Charted Design 176

Enlarging Patterns 177

Blocking Needlework 178

Counted Cross Stitch 179

    Evenweave Fabrics 179
    Embroidery Hoops 180
    Thread 180
    Needles 181
    Methods of Stitching 181
    Cross Stitch on Canvas 182

Needlepoint 183

    Canvas 183
    Frames 184
    Yarns... 184
    Needles 185
    Threading the Needle 185
    Methods of Stitchng 186
    Begin! 187

Following a Stitch Diagram 187

Stitch Dictionary 188

Index 192

Working from a Charted Design

Please note that the words graph and chart are used interchangeably. They mean the same thing. The most important thing to remember in working with a charted design is that each square on the graph represents one stitch.

To determine the size of a finished piece that will be worked by following a graph, count the squares in the height and width of the design. Some of the charts in this book have twelve squares to the inch, with a darker line every sixth intersection, and some have ten squares to the inch, with every fifth intersection line darker. No matter how many squares there are in an inch on the graph, the design can be stitched on a canvas or fabric of any mesh you choose. (Mesh is the number of stitches allowed for in an inch of fabric or canvas.) A design charted on graph paper with 12 squares to the inch may be stitched on 10-mesh needlepoint canvas, 22-mesh hardanger cloth, 14-mesh Aida cloth, 5-mesh quickpoint canvas, or any other mesh canvas or cloth that you want to use. The fact that the chart shows twelve squares to the inch does not affect the size of the finished work; the number of stitches you work in an inch determines the finished size.

Mathematics can be irritating when you are anxious to begin stitching, but it is necessary. If you do not figure carefully at the outset, you may find that you have bought much more material than you need, or much worse, that your stitches run off the edge of the material. In this case, the whole piece will have to be discarded and begun again. Here is a useful formula:

Number of squares in height of graphed design
divided by
Number of stitches in an inch of needlework
equals
Number of inches high stitched design will be.

The same formula works for determining the width.

When you know how long and how wide your stitched design will be, you must then allow extra material around the edges for background, plus 1 to 1½ inches all around for finishing.

Example: A charted design counts 120 squares high by 84 squares wide. To work in needlepoint on 12-mesh canvas, divide 120 by 12 and 84 by 12. The design will work out to be 10 inches high and 7 inches wide. If you

want an additional 1 inch of background stitches all around, the finished piece will measure 9 by 12 inches. Add 1½ inches for finishing; you will need a piece of canvas that measures 12 by 15 inches.

To work the same design in cross stitch on 22-mesh hardanger cloth, divide 120 by 22 and 84 by 22. Your answer will be 5.45 inches high and 3.8 inches wide. Round off the figures to 5½ by 4 inches. If you want an additional ½ inch all around for background material, the finished piece will measure approximately 6½ by 5 inches. Add 1½ inches all around for finishing and you know you will need a piece of hardanger cloth that measures 9½ by 8 inches.

To begin stitching from a charted design, remember that one square on the graph paper represents one stitch. If you have never worked from a chart, your first look at so many small squares of different colors or color symbols may discourage you. There are ways to make counting the squares in the charts easier. A stitch finder can be used with the charts; it has metal strips that you line up underneath the row of squares you are counting. If you do not purchase a stitch finder, you can use a strip of poster paper in the same way. A standing, clear plastic book holder is also an asset, because your angle of vision on a chart is much better when the chart is upright than when it is lying down.

Charts can be either solid colored, color coded, or both. There are advantages to each type of chart. A colored chart will give you a much better idea of how the finished piece will look, but it is sometimes difficult to see the lines of the chart. A color-coded chart has a symbol to represent each color in the design. If the color code indicates that the symbol **X** stands for gold, make a gold stitch for each **X** on the chart. Some color-coded charts are drawn in color—a green X stands for dark green, a green O stands for light green, and so on. In this case, be sure to read the key carefully before you begin stitching.

Some experienced needleworkers help themselves count on a color-coded chart by marking lightly with a pencil those squares they have worked. When the needlework is finished, the pencil markings can be erased so that the chart may be used again.

Work from the center out. Begin counting at the center of the chart and stitching at the center of the material. Usually it is easier to work up from the center and complete the upper part of the design, then finish the lower part. However, it may be easier to outline a central figure beginning with, or close to, the center stitch. Then fill in upper portions of the design, followed by the lower portions.

Find the middle of the chart by counting the number of squares up the height and the number of squares across the width. The place where the exact center of these lines cross each other is the center of the chart. Mark the center point of the chart.

Find the center of your canvas or cloth by folding it in half lengthwise, then again crosswise. Mark the center of the canvas or cloth. The safest method is with a sewing thread that can be snipped out after the work is begun. If you use a pencil, use it lightly. Never use a felt-tipped marker because it will bleed through the needlework.

The center of the chart may fall on one square of the design, or it may be somewhere in the background stitches. The center of the chart is not the same as the center of the design. You will, however, begin stitching from the center of the design. See Figures 1, 2, and 3 for how to start working a design from the center.

After the first stitch, work stitches to the right, left, or up, counting squares on the chart that are the same color and working the same number of squares in the same places on the canvas or cloth.

Enlarging Patterns

It is seldom that you find a pattern that is exactly the size you need. Do not let this inhibit your creativity; enlarging or reducing a pattern is quite simple.

The easiest way to enlarge a pattern is to have it photostatically enlarged. Simply instruct the photostat company as to what size you want the pattern to be. The cost will vary, but this service is usually only available in large towns and cities.

You can easily enlarge or reduce a pattern yourself by using ¼-inch graph paper. You should be able to tell in advance whether or not the design you want to enlarge will fit on one sheet of paper, or whether you must tape several pieces together to get the area you need.

First trace the design you wish to enlarge onto graph paper. If the design is to be twice as large, use two blocks for every one block on the original. Copy carefully, transferring what is in each square to the larger scale. It is helpful sometimes to outline the design with a series of dots, then connect the dots using your straight-edge and French curve to make the lines smooth. Study the following simple examples.

Suppose you want to enlarge a hexagon pattern. (Figure 4.) On the original scale, each block equals ¼ inch. To make it twice as large, each space that is presently contained in one block must be stretched to two. The length of

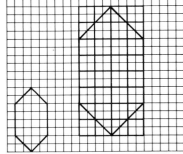

Figure 4

the original hexagon from end to end is eight squares; the width is four squares. When enlarged, the length should be sixteen squares and the width eight. Count off sixteen in length and eight in width on graph paper as shown. Draw the lengthwise and crosswise lines every two blocks to give yourself a larger scale. Draw the hexagon onto the new scale, transferring exactly to the larger squares what is in each of the smaller squares.

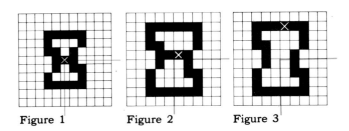

Figure 1   Figure 2   Figure 3

Figure 1. If the center of the chart is one square, begin by making that stitch.

Figure 2. If the center is a point where four stitches meet, choose either of the upper two squares and begin stitching.

Figure 3. If the center of the chart falls on the background, count up to the nearest design square and begin stitching there.

Irregular shapes are just as easily enlarged. Draw your new scale onto your graph paper, then copy exactly what is in each of the smaller squares. (Figure 5.)

Regular shapes such as diamonds or squares can be enlarged by merely extending the sides with a straightedge to the desired length. (Figure 6.)

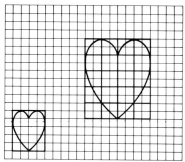

Figure 5

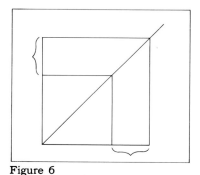

Figure 6

Blocking Needlework

The purpose of blocking is to pull the threads of the canvas or fabric on which the needlework was done back to their original "on grain" position. Keep in mind that, while blocking can make up for a multitude of mistakes made while working the piece, it cannot correct entirely a piece that has been worked so tightly that the canvas is stretched permanently out of shape. The moral is to work with an even, slightly loose tension.

If a needlepoint piece is badly out of shape, it must be soaked in cold water. This step is to be avoided if possible, especially if a painted canvas was used. The colors of the painted canvas may bleed, not because of the paint or ink, most of which is guaranteed not to run, but because of the very necessary sizing that comes loose from the canvas and floats the colors through the piece. If a piece must be soaked, be sure to dry it flat, rather than upright, to give less chance of the colors bleeding onto one another.

Alternative methods for dampening a piece before pinning it to the blocking board are rolling it in a wet towel until the piece is damp, or spraying it with water. Steam pressing your work with a wet cloth after the piece is pinned down is usually enough for pieces that are not much out of shape, as is often the case with bargello and pieces worked on a frame or hoop.

The steps to be followed in pinning down a needlework piece are always the same except that wet pieces should be blocked right side up and pieces to be steamed should be blocked upside down. (The reason for this is to retain stitch texture and prevent flattening the face of the work.) Pinning down may be done on a plywood board or a cutting board. If the piece is small, the ironing board may be used.

First mark a square or rectangle the size of the canvas on the board or on paper attached to the board. (If you do a lot of blocking, it will be useful to mark a board in 1-inch squares across the whole surface so that pieces of many different sizes can be blocked on the board.) Aluminum push pins are the best to use for blocking because they are sharp and do not rust. Two precautions: make certain your pins are rustproof, and never pin into the worked part of the canvas.

Most needlepoint requiring blocking has become slightly diamond shaped. To correct this, pin the needlepoint to the marked board as follows: Starting at A, pin the corner to the board at the upper left corner. Place a pin at 1 and 2 in the same corner. At opposite corner B, repeat the procedure through 3 and 4. Now pin from 2 toward C, spacing pins about 1 inch apart. Stop the pins about 2 inches from corner C. Repeat from 1 to D, then from D to 4 and C to 3. (Figure 7.)

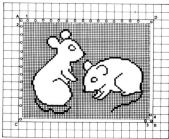

Figure 7

If the piece is soaking wet, allow to dry thoroughly—at least 24 hours. If the piece is face down, use a wet cloth and steam iron until it is damp through and allow to dry thoroughly. Drying is important because the needlepoint will revert to its original warped shape if removed from the blocking board while still wet.

Cross stitch and other embroidery work should be blocked on a heavily padded surface, such as can be formed with several layers of toweling. Work with the embroidery face down. Using a steam iron and a light spray starch, press and pull the embroidery to the correct shape with the backs of your hands. Let it dry in the correct shape before moving it.

Counted Cross Stitch

Although properly called counted cross stitch, this popular form of needlework is also referred to as "thread count" work, which is much too broad a term, and Danish cross stitch.

Cross stitch has almost unlimited versatility and is inexpensive in terms of both money and time involved. Because the fabric serves as the background of the design (as opposed to needlepoint where the background mesh must be filled in with stitches), projects worked in cross stitch are completed much more rapidly than a needlepoint project worked from the same charted design. Any charted needlepoint design is suitable for cross stitch.

EVENWEAVE FABRICS

Evenweave fabrics are those in which the horizontal and vertical threads are woven the same distance apart. Therefore, cross stitches worked over thread intersections on such fabrics are perfectly square stitches.

Although many fabrics may appear to be evenly woven, there are three fabrics that are woven specifically for cross stitch: Evenweave linen, Hardanger cloth, and Aida cloth. These fabrics are sold by the yard, half yard, or in cut pieces, and are available in white, off-white, and ecru. Shops specializing in cross stitch supplies may also have these fabrics in pastels and bright colors. They may seem expensive, but a very small amount of fabric will serve as background for many projects.

The size of the completed cross stitches is determined by the particular fabric selected.

Evenweave linen is a very finely woven cloth. Cross stitches are placed by counting each thread in the cloth as you work. Linen is composed of round threads, which means that the cross stitches are always made over two threads. The most readily available size of evenweave linen is 15 stitches (30 threads) to the inch.

Hardanger cloth is relatively easy to recognize because each vertical and horizontal division is formed by a pair of threads that are woven with an easy-to-see separation. The weave looks like little "squares," and makes stitch placement easy. The most popular size of Hardanger cloth is 22 stitches to the inch. Unlike evenweave linen, Hardanger cloth has flat threads. Cross stitches made on Hardanger cloth should be made over one square of the fabric.

Aida cloth is a basketweave fabric in which each vertical and horizontal division is made up of interlocking threads. Definite holes clearly indicate where each stitch should be worked. Because of the flat threads of the fabric, cross stitches worked on Aida cloth, as with those worked on Hardanger cloth, should be made over one square of the fabric to ensure uniformity of stitches. The most commonly used sizes of Aida cloth are 14 stitches-to-the-inch fine Aida and 11 stitches-to-the-inch coarse Aida.

If you wish to work cross stitch on one of the solid colored, evenweave fabrics mentioned, but prefer not to count threads for each stitch, use the technique outlined for Cross Stitch on Canvas.

Checked gingham is often chosen as the background cloth for cross stitch because the checks provide a ready guide for the stitches. Cross stitch on gingham is a particularly easy technique for beginners. On gingham, the cross stitches are usually placed in the white squares, but interesting variations can be worked when some or all of the stitches are placed in the colored squares.

Always choose fabric that is the proper scale to your design: fine fabric is best for an intricately detailed design with areas of delicate shading; coarser fabrics work well for bolder designs.

A design can be made larger or smaller depending on the size of the fabric on which you work it. A design may also be enlarged by letting each square on the chart equal two or more stitches, both vertically and horizontally. The easiest method of enlargement is to simply work over additional threads on the fabric: stitch over four threads instead of two on linen, and stitch over two threads instead of one for Hardanger and Aida cloth.

Determine the size of your finished project and the amount of fabric needed for finishing by the method described in Working from a Charted Design. If you are working a very small design such as those that fit into key chains or Christmas ornament frames, be sure to leave enough background fabric so that it will fit into your smallest hoop.

Regardless of the fabric you choose or the size of the design, prepare the fabric by basting all cut edges under in a narrow hem, or whip stitch over the edges to keep them from fraying. Another alternative is to run a machine zig-zag stitch around the edges, or stitch double-fold bias tape over them.

EMBROIDERY HOOPS

Most needleworkers prefer to work counted cross stitch with the fabric stretched in a hoop, although some fabrics are stiff enough so that they may be easily worked without a hoop. The greatest advantage of working with a hoop is that your stitch tension will be even.

No matter what size your finished cross-stitched project is to be, you will be working only small areas of the design at a time. Since cross stitches are not marred by placing the hoop over areas you have already worked, it is best to work with a very small hoop—4 or 5 inches in diameter.

The better hoops are wood or plastic and are made with a screw-type tension adjuster as opposed to the spring types that make it more difficult to maintain proper tension on the fabric.

If you are right-handed, position your hoop on the fabric so that the screw adjustment is at 10 o'clock; 2 o'clock works best if you are left-handed. This will keep your thread from becoming entangled in the screw. Keep the selvages to the side, rather than at the top and bottom.

To stretch your fabric on a hoop, first adjust the screw so that the outside ring fits snugly over the inside ring and material. (Figure 8.) Never alter the screw once the fabric and hoop are in place.

Pull the material taut. (Figure 9.) If the outside ring is tight enough, the fabric will not slip.

When the fabric is taut, push the outside ring down. (Figure 10.) To release the fabric, do not alter the tension screw, but press thumbs firmly against the fabric on the hoop while lifting the outside ring up and off.

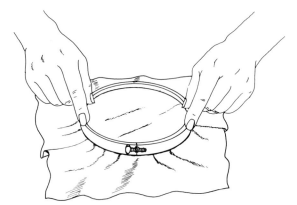
Figure 8

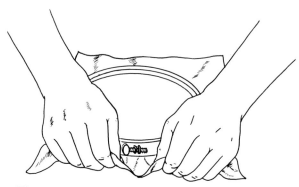
Figure 9

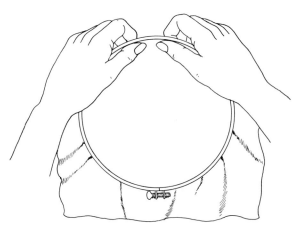
Figure 10

During the course of stitching, you may find it necessary to tug at the fabric every now and then to keep it taut within the frame. Always remove the fabric from the hoop before putting your work away.

THREAD

Six-strand mercerized cotton floss is an excellent choice for working cross stitch. Hundreds of colors are available, including many different hues of the same color, which enables you to work intricate shadings into your designs. The six-strand cotton floss is usually available in 9-yard skeins. Each thread may be divided so that you can work with any number of strands.

Perle cotton, also widely used in cross stitch, is a glossy, twisted thread that is thicker than mercerized cotton. The two sizes of Perle cotton most suitable for cross stitch are size 5 that comes in 53-yard balls, and size 8 that is available in 95-yard balls.

Danish flower thread is a beautiful cotton floss that is slightly heavier than most mercerized cottons.

Cross stitch on wool evenweave fabrics and on some of the coarser cotton fabrics may be worked with crewel wool or one strand of Persian wool.

Experiment to see how many strands of thread to use on a given fabric. Generally speaking, the following guidelines are good to remember: On medium-weight linen (30 threads or 15 stitches to the inch) and fine Aida cloth (14 stitches to the inch), use two strands of regular floss or one strand of Danish flower thread. On 22-mesh Hardanger cloth, work with one strand of cotton embroidery floss. Coarse Aida cloth (11 stitches to the inch) is best worked with three or four strands of cotton floss or two strands of Danish flower thread, or one or two strands of Persian yarn or crewel wool.

If you prefer more texture in your designs, try increasing the number of strands you use.

Cut the thread into 18- to 20-inch lengths. Longer strands tend to twist as you work.

NEEDLES

One of the most important things to remember when working with evenweave fabrics is that the needle should *never* pierce the fabric; instead it should slip through the openings *between* the threads of the fabric. For this reason, a blunt-tipped tapestry needle is used. The sizes that are most appropriate for working cross stitch are 24, 25, and 26. The higher the needle number, the smaller the needle. The size needle you use will depend on how finely your fabric is woven and what thread you've chosen to use.

Experienced needleworkers have found that even the most expensive tapestry needles tend to rust or discolor from the moisture in your hands and in the air. For this reason, it is a good rule never to leave your needle in your fabric when you are not stitching.

Thread the needle for cross stitch just as you would for other types of crewel embroidery. (See "Threading the Needle" in the Needlepoint section of this Appendix.)

METHODS OF STITCHING

Designs for counted cross stitch are always charted. Each square of the chart represents a counted square of fabric, and each symbol in a graph square represents one stitch. The symbols in the squares are often keyed to color schemes, or the colors in the squares indicate the color thread to use.

Cross stitch may be worked in horizontal rows, vertical rows, or diagonal rows, depending on the design you are stitching. There are two methods of working cross stitches. You may either work all of the under stitches first and then go back and cross each (Figures 11 and 12), or you may complete each cross before proceeding on to the next. (Figure 13.)

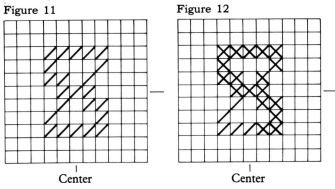

Figure 11   Figure 12

Center   Center

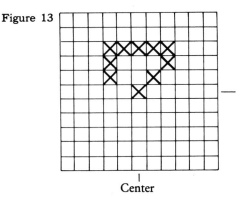

Figure 13

Center

In cross stitch, each under stitch of the cross should slant in the same direction, and the crossing upper stitch should slant consistently in the opposite direction. Note that each stitch interlocks, or "holds hands" with its neighboring stitches. The same hole is often used more than once; four times is the usual in a solidly cross-stitched area of a design.

The "punch-and-stab" method of stitching described in the section on Needlepoint is a better stitching method for cross stitch than the "needle-through" or sewing method, also described under Needlepoint. With the punch-and-stab method, each thread lies flat with just the right tension. If the needle-through method is used, the stitches can easily be pulled too tightly, thereby distorting the holes of the fabric.

It is best to begin stitching at the top of a design area and work down. In this manner the needle moves up in an empty space and down into a used space, which is easier than bringing the needle up in a used space.

Starting a New Strand of Thread. With each new strand of floss, leave a 1-inch tail of thread on the back of your fabric, holding it in place with your finger. Work your first stitches over this tail to secure it. (Figure 14 .) Never knot your thread; it might show through as an ugly irregularity once the finished design is framed or mounted.

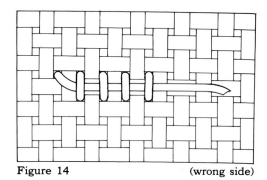

Figure 14   (wrong side)

Ending a Strand of Thread. To end each thread color, bring your needle to the back of the fabric and run it under the stitches in the last row you worked, being careful not to pull the thread too tightly. For extra security, make a loop over the last stitch and draw the needle through once. (Figure 15.) Cut the thread without leaving a tail. Whenever possible, end a thread by traveling in the same direction in which you were working.

Never carry long threads from one area of the design to another. Instead, work the needle under the stitches on the back of the fabric to the new position, or end the strand and begin a new one in the new position.

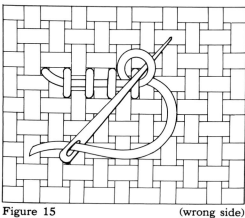

Figure 15   (wrong side)

Additional Stitches. Two other stitches are useful in cross stitching: the half cross and the backstitch.

The half cross stitch is exactly that: one-half of a cross stitch. Depending on your design needs, the half cross may slant either to the right or to the left.

The backstitch is used quite a bit in cross stitch (as in needlepoint) for details. It allows you to move more freely on the fabric than either the cross or the half cross stitch. Although it is always worked from hole to hole, backstitching can run up, down, across, or diagonally. Use backstitching to outline a design area in contrasting or complementary colors for a dramatic effect, or to emphasize a design area that might otherwise fade into the background. You can also work backstitches over cross stitching for small details such as facial features or flower centers. Be conservative in the use of backstitching, however, or your design could assume a "coloring book" effect.

CROSS STITCH ON CANVAS

Historically, this technique was used extensively in the 1920s when cross stitch was a favorite form of needlework. This technique eliminates counting fabric threads and assures uniformity of stitches on a solid-colored background cloth. Although it is being done today with kits, cross stitch on canvas can easily be done with a few materials and the charted designs in this book. Follow the steps outlined below.

First position your fabric in the hoop as discussed in the section on Embroidery Hoops.

Cut a piece of waste-thread canvas to the size necessary to cover the area of your design within the hoop. Waste-thread canvas is manufactured especially for cross stitch on canvas. It is soft, has very little sizing in it, and every fifth thread is blue to help you count. Regular needlepoint canvas will not work for this technique because of the stiffness of the mesh.

Prepare the canvas as for needlepoint by taping all four edges to keep them from raveling.

Baste the prepared canvas to the right side of your fabric, aligning the grain of the canvas with the fabric grain. (Figure 16 .)

Work your design in cross stitch, stitching over the canvas mesh through the fabric. Make all stitches in the punch-and-stab method discussed earlier.

When the design is completely worked in cross stitch, remove the tape from the edges of the canvas and pull out the canvas threads one by one (tweezers may be helpful). (Figure 17.) If the threads of the canvas prove difficult to remove, dampen the work with a sponge to soften the sizing of the canvas.

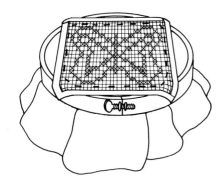

Figure 16

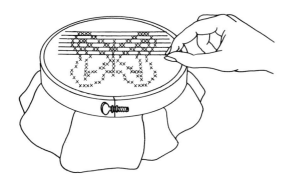

Figure 17

Needlepoint

Exquisitely elegant and at the same time extremely durable, needlepoint is the acknowledged aristocrat of the decorative needle arts. A form of counted thread embroidery, it is worked over and completely covers a grid formed by the evenly woven threads of a canvas backing. It is a medium that offers a broad range of creative alternatives, and it requires little by way of tools and equipment.

CANVAS

There are three different kinds of needlepoint canvas (not including the plastic variety). Sold by the yard, they are made in a number of different sizes and widths, and usually in two colors—white and ecru. Size is determined by the number of mesh, or threads, per running inch. The fewer the number of threads, the larger the holes between them, and thus the heavier the yarns you will need to cover the canvas.

The various mesh sizes are generally divided into three categories: the finest mesh canvases, 16 or more mesh per inch, are used for petit point work; the middle range, from about 8 to 15 mesh per inch, are called gros point; and the largest mesh, from 3 to 7 threads per inch, are known as quick point.

Mono canvas consists of single vertical (warp) threads crossing single horizontal (weft) threads. It is an evenly woven, sturdy, all-purpose canvas, but since the threads are not interlocked, it tends to pull out of shape when worked and may require repeated blocking. Mono canvas comes in various sizes from 10 to 24 mesh per inch. Available widths range from 36 to 60 inches.

Interlock canvas, at first glance, looks like mono canvas with single vertical and horizontal threads. It differs from mono canvas, however, in that the mesh actually consists of groups of threads that are twisted at each intersection, thus locking the canvas in place and preventing the threads from shifting as you stitch.

Penelope canvas is woven with pairs of vertical and horizontal threads, the vertical ones spaced closely together and the horizontal ones slightly farther apart. The threads of penelope canvas are usually somewhat finer and flatter than those of a similar size mono canvas. On penelope canvas, stitches can be worked over pairs of threads, or the threads may be separated and finer detail can be stitched over individual threads. The size of penelope canvas is usually indicated by a set of two numbers, the first indicating the number of stitches per inch that can be made when working over pairs of threads, the second referring to the number of stitches per inch that can be made if the canvas threads are separated and stitches are worked over individual threads. Penelope canvas is made in 40- and 60-inch widths and in sizes as fine as 14/28 mesh.

Plastic mesh "canvas" is also a suitable backing for needlepoint. One virtue of stitching on a plastic mesh foundation is that it will never shift out of shape and thus will never require blocking. It is somewhat thicker than ordinary cotton canvas and comes in fewer sizes.

Always cut your canvas at least 1 to 1½ inches larger on all four sides than the size of your finished piece. Mark the top of your canvas.

To prepare your canvas, bind all cut edges (selvages need not be bound) with masking tape on both the back and front sides of the canvas. This will keep the edges from raveling as you work.

FRAMES

It is not essential to stretch the canvas mesh backing used to needlepoint on a frame. Many people prefer to work with the canvas in their hands. Frames reduce the portability of your needlepoint work, but they do keep the canvas from pulling out of shape.

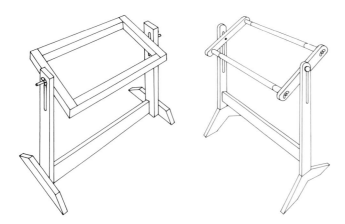

Figure 18

Large adjustable easel-type frames or hoops—either floor-standing or table model (Figure 18)—can be tilted to any angle, raised and lowered, and many collapse for storage. Some of the rectangular models are fitted with adjustable rollers at the top and bottom of the frame, which simplifies the task of moving the finished part of the needlepoint piece out of the way when you want to work on a new section. For small projects, a large embroidery hoop with a thumbscrew will do just as well. (Figure 19.)

Figure 19

When using a small frame for a large needlepoint project, you simply move the work from section to section, reattaching it to the frame when you want to work on a new portion.

YARNS

Generally speaking, yarns for needlepoint should be durable. The best yarns are made of wool (though there are some suitable synthetics), have long, tough fibers, and are tightly spun—all of which gives them the hard finish and resiliency needed for any rough treatment they will receive. In addition, needlepoint yarns should be colorfast and mothproofed. There are several yarns that meet these requirements admirably, notably the Persian, tapestry, rya, and rug yarns. They differ in weight and thickness, in number of ply and type of twist, and in the range of colors available.

Crewel yarns and Nantucket twist, along with various cotton, silk, rayon, and metallic embroidery flosses are also used for many types of needlepoint projects. Knitting yarns should never be used to make a needlepoint project: they are too soft and springy and will fuzz up and fray when pulled through the canvas.

Six-strand embroidery floss gives a striking effect when used for petit point, but its use should be restricted to canvas of small enough mesh so that the floss completely covers the canvas.

Persian yarn. A wool yarn with a lustrous sheen, Persian is one of the highest quality and most popular of all the needlepoint yarns. Each full strand is made of three loosely twisted individual two-ply strands that can be worked as one or separated and used individually. A full strand (three individual strands together, that is) will cover 10-mesh canvas well, and two full strands work satisfactorily on 7-mesh canvas. Three or more full strands can be used together on the 3- to 5-mesh canvases, but on these sizes the heavier rya and rug yarns are easier to work with. Persian yarns come in an almost bewildering array of vibrant colors. (Paternayan, for example, dyes its fine line of Persian yarns in 343 different shades.) They are sold in skeins of different sizes from little 8- or 9-yard packets to large 8-ounce skeins. Some stores will sell quantities as small as a single 30-inch strand.

Tapestry yarn. A tightly twisted four-ply wool yarn, tapestry yarn is slightly heavier than a full strand of Persian yarn. The two are often used interchangeably, although the ply of tapestry yarn cannot be separated into individual strands and the range of colors available is somewhat more limited. One strand works well on 10-mesh canvas and two strands will cover a 7-mesh canvas. Tapestry yarns are readily available in small 8- to 9-yard skeins; some manufacturers also package 100-yard skeins, although these are harder to find.

Rug yarn. The heaviest of the needlepoint yarns, these are often called "quick point" yarns because they are used with the largest mesh canvases and work up very quickly. Rug yarns range from two- to six-ply and come in different types of twists from quite smooth to rather rope-like. Some are just a bit thicker than tapestry yarn and work well on a 7-mesh canvas, while others are extremely bulky and will fill the 3- to 5-mesh canvases beautifully. The range of colors available varies with the particular manufacturer and the line of yarn; some are made in 40 or 50 colors, while others come in more than 200 different shades.

Yarns are dyed in batches, called dye lots, and the same color often varies from one dye lot to another (except for tapestry yarn, which is dyed very uniformly and always seems to match). With the other yarns, however, it is important to buy all you will need of each color—and a little extra for good measure—at the same time. Always check to make sure that all the skeins of each color are marked with the same dye lot number.

All you have to do to prepare yarns for use is to cut it into strands about 30 inches long. Some yarns are packaged in pull skeins, in which case just pull out, measure, and cut a batch of 30-inch lengths. To keep the different colors from getting mixed up, make a loose knot in the middle of each batch.

NEEDLES

Needlepoint work is always done with tapestry needles, which are longish, blunt-tipped needles with large oval eyes. The blunt tip is important in order to avoid splitting the yarn or the threads of the backing, so do not substitute sharp-tipped needles. Tapestry needles come in a dozen different numbered sizes, ranging from size 13 for the largest and longest ones, to size 24 for the shortest and most slender. The needle should be able to slip through the canvas mesh easily, without distorting it, but at the same time must have a large enough eye so the yarn can be threaded without fraying. Thus, the size needle you will need will depend on the mesh size of the canvas you plan to use and the thickness of the yarn. The larger, or lower numbered needle should be used with the large (lower numbered) mesh canvases and heavier yarns. The relatively finer, higher numbered needles are appropriate for the higher numbered, smaller mesh canvases and thinner yarns. Fine petit point, for example, worked on a 24-mesh-to-the-inch canvas, requires size 24 needles; 10-mesh canvas is usually worked with size 18 needles, 7-mesh canvas with sizes 16 to 18 needles, and the 3- to 5-mesh canvases with jumbo size 13 needles.

THREADING THE NEEDLE

Sometimes trying to thread the ends of heavy yarns through the slender eye of a needle can be exasperating. There are several tricks you can use, however, to overcome this obstacle.

Method 1. Fold the end of the yarn over the needle and pinch the fold tightly between your thumb and index finger. (Figure 20.) Slide the needle out and push the eye over the folded yarn, using a sawing motion to help it slide over the yarn. (Figure 21.) Then pull the yarn through with your fingers.

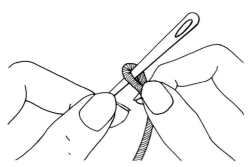

Figure 20

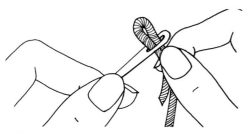

Figure 21

Method 2. Cut a strip of paper slightly narrower in width than the size of the needle eye. Fold the paper in half and slip the yarn end into the fold. Insert the narrow cut ends of the paper strip into the needle eye, and then pull the paper and yarn through the eye. (Figure 22.)

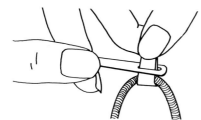

Figure 22

METHODS OF STITCHING

The canvas is usually worked with the selvages at the sides, that is, with the vertical (warp) threads of the canvas running straight away from you; but it is frequently rotated 180 degrees (turned so the bottom becomes the top and the top becomes the bottom) to work alternating rows of stitches.

If your canvas is a large one, roll up the end

you aren't working on and secure it with a few safety pins to keep it out of your way. Pin it in the margins so that you will not distort the canvas mesh within the design area or snag any stitches you may have already completed.

There are two different ways to insert the needle into the canvas to form any given needlepoint stitch. Many needlepointers prefer the faster and more ryhthmic single motion of the "needle-through" technique as a general purpose method of stitching, reserving the slower, two-motion "punch-and-stab" technique for special circumstances—as when working with the canvas stretched on a frame, when the direction in which the needle must be pointed to form a particular stitch is an awkward one or one that will push the canvas threads out of line. There are no hard and fast rules that must be followed in selecting one or the other method: just remember that you should feel comfortable stitching, and your stitches should be plump and even and should distort the canvas as little as possible.

With both methods, a uniform tension should be maintained, one that is not so tight that the canvas will become misshapen or so loose that the stitches themselves will be malformed and uneven.

Needle-Through Method. In this method, one stitch is completed and the next one begun in a single operation. To begin, bring the needle up from the wrong side of the canvas in the hole where you wish to start your first stitch (this is usually referred to as the base of the stitch), and pull the yarn through. Then, in one continuous motion, simply insert the needle from front to back (that is, from the right side to the wrong side), into the canvas at the top of the first stitch, slide the needle along the underside of the canvas, and bring it out in the hole that will form the base of the next stitch, drawing the yarn all the way through as you pull the needle out. This will tighten the first stitch and begin a new one at the same time. Repeat the procedure to make each succeeding stitch.

Punch-and-Stab Method. In this method, the needle is inserted into the canvas and then brought out again in two distinctly separate motions. Holding the needle perpendicular to the canvas, punch it through from underneath, then switch your hand to the front of the canvas and pull the needle through, drawing the yarn all the way through. Then stab the needle straight down into the canvas in the next hole appropriate for the stitch you are making, switch your hand to the underside of the canvas, and pull needle and yarn all the way through. Repeat the two operations for all succeeding stitches.

Starting a New Strand of Yarn. Yarn can be anchored several ways. After you have finished the first strand, try to stagger the beginnings and endings so that they don't fall at the same spot on each row.

Method 1. This method can be used to start the first strand or to begin new strands once the work is in progess. Bring the yarn up from the back of the canvas in the first hole of your stitch pattern, leaving an end about 1 inch long on the wrong side of the canvas. Point this end in the direction in which you will be stitching and hold it flat against the canvas with one hand. Then work your stitches over the yarn end, fastening it securely against the back of the canvas.

Method 2. This method can also be used to anchor the first strand of yarn or new strands once the work is in progress. Knot the end of the yarn and insert the needle through the canvas from front to back (right side to wrong side) about 1 inch away in the direction you will be working from the first hole of your stitch pattern. Then bring the needle up from the back in the first hole of your stitch and work the stitches over the yarn end. When you approach the knot, trim it away and push the short end to the back of the work. Since knots are never left in a finished piece of needlepoint, do not stitch over them or forget to trim them away.

Ending a Strand of Yarn. When only 3 or 4 inches of the strand you are working with remain, or when you need to end one color and begin another, bring the needle through to the wrong side of the work and weave the yarn for about 1 inch through the backs of the adjacent stitches. Then trim the excess yarn close to the canvas. Avoid weaving dark color yarns through light ones wherever possible.

To avoid having to end a strand of yarn and start it again in a nearby area, you can carry yarn across the back of the canvas to begin working in a new spot. But if the area you are finishing and the one you are about to start are more than ½ inch apart, weave the yarn through the back of the work in the intervening space to avert potential snags.

BEGIN!

There are no absolute rules about how you must go about stitching your needlepoint project. Every design is different and the order of work will vary with the nature of the design. There are some guide lines, however, that experienced needlepointers have found to be helpful. Generally the design area is worked first, then the background and borders, if any. Within the design itself, start by completing all the fine lines and details; you won't be able to find them if you stitch in the areas around them first. Some people like to stitch any areas with subtly graded shading next, because once too many colors have been worked into the canvas it becomes difficult to distinguish the closely related shades. Thereafter, you can complete small segments of the design and then go on to the larger ones, or work color by color, as you prefer. In either case, however, it is wise to work the dark tones first and leave the lighter colors for last. Your needlepoint piece will stay cleaner longer this way.

Work complete rows wherever possible. Don't jump around because if you work little blocks of background here and there, you will find that there will be faint but unsightly lines and ridges where the blocks come together.

When you have finished your needlepoint project, check to make sure that you haven't missed any stitches by holding the piece up to the light. If you spot any missed stitches, fill them in if you can do so unobtrusively. After you have done this, weave any remaining loose yarn ends into the back of the work for an inch or so and trim away the excess.

Following a Stitch Diagram

Instructions for working needlepoint stitches are usually presented in diagram form. The order in which the needle is to go in and out of the canvas is usually indicated by a series of consecutive numbers appearing at each end of every stitch. To follow any stitch diagram, the needle is always brought up from underneath on odd numbers (1, 3, 5, etc.), and inserted from front to back (right side to wrong side) on even numbers (2, 4, 6, etc.). When the numbers along a row of stitches are printed upside down, it means that in order to work the stitches along that particular row, the canvas is to be rotated 180 degrees so that the top edge is at the bottom and the bottom edge is at the top.

Stitch Dictionary

Basic Stitches

Basketweave
or Diagonal Tent Stitch

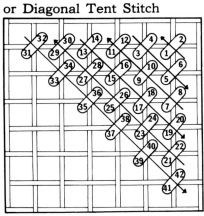

Continental or Tent Stitch
horizontal

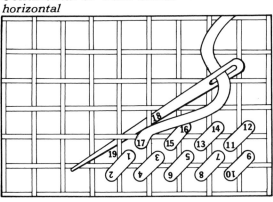

vertical

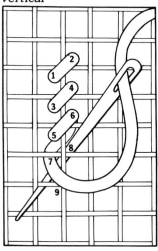

Decorative Stitches

Back Stitch

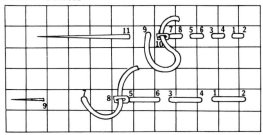

Cashmere Stitch

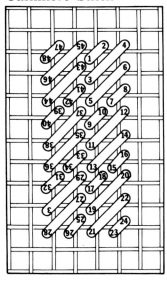

Ridged Cashmere Stitch

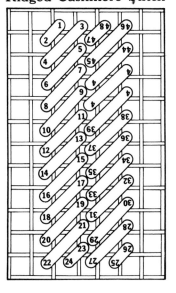

Brick Stitch

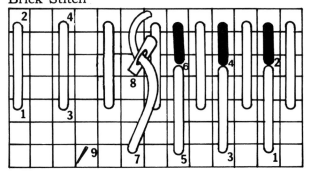

Checker Stitch

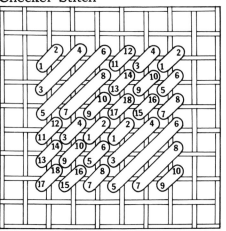

Byzantine Stitch

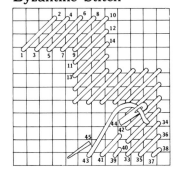

Cross Stitch *method 1*

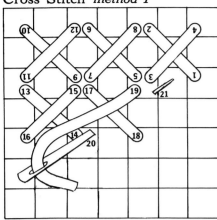

method 2

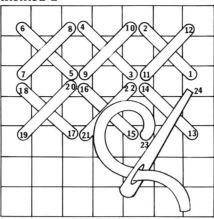

Half Cross Stitch

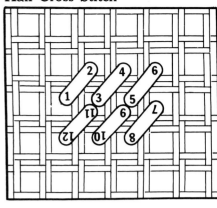

Long-Armed Cross Stitch

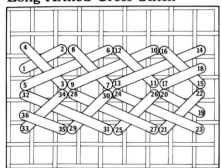

Smyrna Cross Stitch

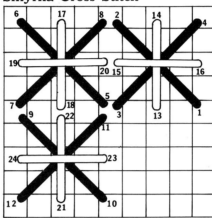

Upright Cross Stitch

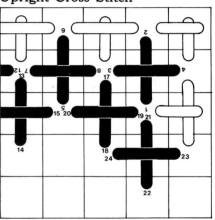

Eyelet Stitch

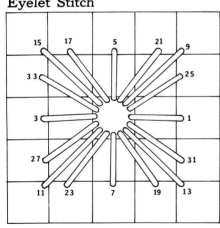

Eyelet Stitch (variation)

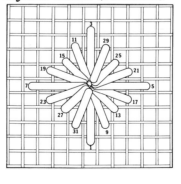

Fern Stitch

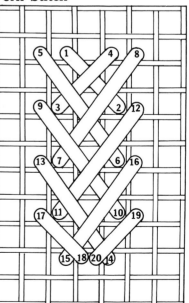

Jacquard Stitch

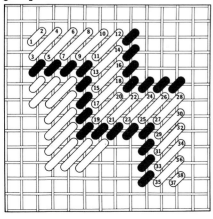

Kalem or Knitting Stitch

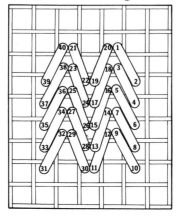

Encroaching Gobelin Stitch

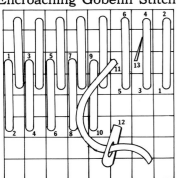

Slanted Gobelin Stitch

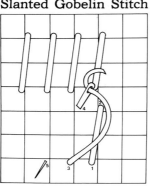

Slanted Encroaching Gobelin Stitch

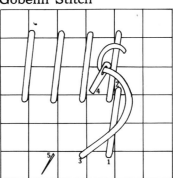

Upright Gobelin Stitch

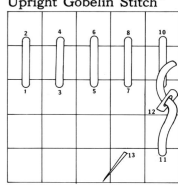

Knotted Stitch

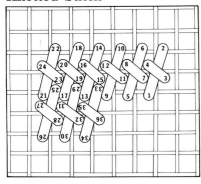

Mosaic Stitch *in progress*   *finished effect*

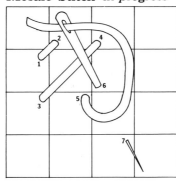
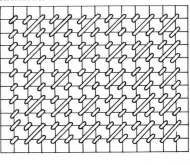

Continuous or Diagonal Mosaic Stitch

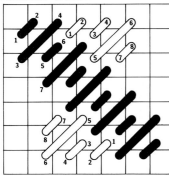

Scotch, Flat, or Diagonal Satin Stitch

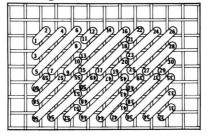

Checkerboard Scotch Stitch

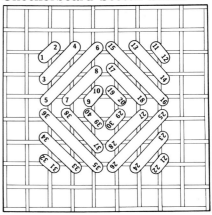

Outlined Scotch Stitch

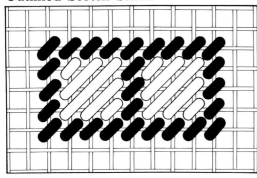

Stem Stitch with Backstitching

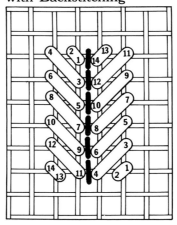

Vandyke Stitch

Leaf Stitch *in progress*

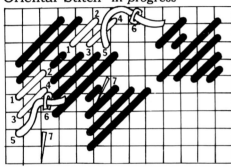

finished effect

Alternating Scotch Stitch
in progress

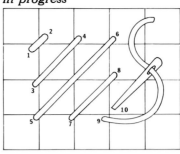

finished effect

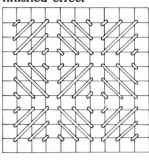

Oriental Stitch *in progress*

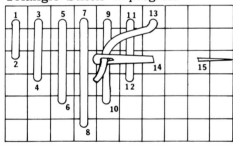

finished effect

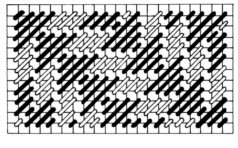

Hungarian Ground Stitch

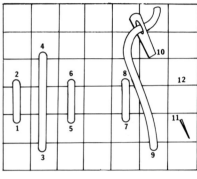

Triangle Stitch *in progress*

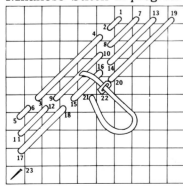

finished effect

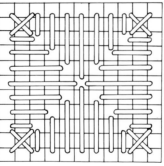

Woven Stitch *step 1*

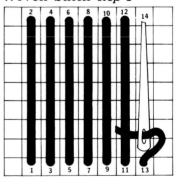

Milanese Stitch *in progress*

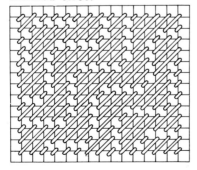

finished effect

step 2

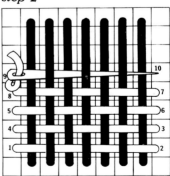

Index

A

Aida cloth, 179, 181
Alphabets (varied styles), 125, 155-173
Alternating scotch stitch, 191
Angels
    praying, 50, 66
    trumpeting, 59, 67
Animals, 99, 113-128

B

Backgammon board, bargello, 106-107
Back stitch, 188
Backstitching, 182
    with stem stitch, 190
Balloons, 53
Bargello backgammon board, 106-107
Basketweave stitch, 188
Bear, 119, 160
Bibles, 90, 94
Birds, 9-24, 73-75, 77, 79, 142-160
Blocking needlework, 178-179
Brick stitch, 188
Bridge patterns, 104, 108, 109
Bull, 62
Butterflies, 25, 26, 72, 142, 162
Byzantine stitch, 188

C

Camels, 99
Candelabra, 84
Canvas
    cross stitch on, 179, 182-183
    interlock, 183
    mesh, 176, 183
    mono, 183
    needle sizes for, 185
    penelope, 183-184
    preparing, 183, 184
    waste-thread, 182
Caribbean, 136
Cashmere stitch, 188
    ridged, 188
Castles, 134
Cats, 118, 119, 128
Charted design, working from a, 176-177
Chalice, 90
Checkerboard, 110-111
Checkerboard scotch stitch, 190
Checker stitch, 188
Chess board, 110-111
Chick, 72
Children, designs for, 47-58
Child's illustrated alphabet, 156-164
Chipmunk, 118
Christ Child, 69
Christmas designs, 66-71

Clown, 160
Coat of arms, 153
Continental stitch, 188
Continuous mosaic stitch, 190
Cotton floss, 180-181
Counted cross stitch, 179-183
Cows, 68, 118, 119
Crab, 63
Cross stitch
    counted, 179-183
    for needlepoint, 189
    half, 189
    long-armed, 189
    on canvas, 182-183
    smyrna, 189
    upright, 189
Crosses, 85, 86, 89, 90, 92
Crowns, 86, 90

D

Danish flower thread, 181
Dart board, 108-109
Deer, 78, 99, 114, 118
Diagonal mosaic stitch, 190
Diagonal satin stitch, 190
Diagonal tent stitch, 188
Dice, 112
Dogs, 119, 161
Donkey, 68
Doves, 69, 79, 85, 90, 98
Dragon, 56
Drum, 79
Ducks, 78

E

Eagles, 20, 21, 74-75
Easter, 72, 77
Eggs, 72, 77, 158
Elephants, 99, 126
Embroidery hoops, 180, 182, 183
Encroaching gobelin stitch, 190
Enlarging patterns, 177-178, 179
Evenweave fabrics, 179
    on a hoop, 180
    needles for, 181
    stitching on, 181
Evenweave linen, 179, 181
Eyelet stitch, 189

F

Ferns, 42
Fern stitch, 189
Fish, 60, 78, 91, 93
Flag, 74-75, 77
Flat stitch, 190
Fleur de lis, 102
Flowers, 27-46, 52-53,

77, 156, 160
Following a stitch diagram, 187
Four seasons, 76-79
Fourth of July, 74-75
Frames
    baby's, 51
    for cross stitch, 180
    for needlepoint, 184
    seashells, 151
    wedding, 80
Fruit, 139, 142

G

Gamecock, 24
Games, 103-112
Geometric designs, 139, 140, 143-145, 148-150, 152, 154, 162, 163
Gingerbread man, 53
Gingham, cross stitch on checked, 179
Giraffes, 99, 113, 127
Goat, 60
Gobelin stitch
    encroaching, 190
    slanted, 190
    upright, 190
Grape vine, 6-8

H

Half cross stitch, 182, 189
Hardanger cloth, 179, 181
Hearts, 76, 104, 108-109
Horses, 79, 99, 118, 122
Hungarian ground stitch, 191

I

Illuminated letters, 170-173
Indian chief, 54
Indian patterns, 55

J

Jack, 104, 108-109
Jacquard stitch, 189
Joseph, 68

K

Kalem stitch, 189
Kite, 76
Kings, 71, 104, 108-109
Knitting stitch, 189
Knotted stitch, 190

L

Ladybugs, 142
Lamp, 90, 94
Leaf stitch, 191
Leaves, 150
Lions, 63, 87, 99, 120-121, 158
    Aztec, 146-147

Long-armed cross stitch, 189
Lord's prayer, 88
Lute, 79

M

Maps, 137, 138
Milanese stitch, 191
Monkeys, 116-117, 156, 160
Months, 76-79
Mosaic stitch, 190
    continuous, 190
    diagonal, 190
Mother's Day, 65
Mountains, 132, 134

N

Nativity scene, 68-71
Needlepoint, 183-191
    stitch diagrams, 188-191. See also specific stitch.
Needles
    for cross stitch, 181
    for needlepoint, 185
Needle-through stitching, 182

O

Ocean wave, 133
Oriental figures, 129, 130, 132
Oriental stitch, 191
Outlined scotch stitch, 190
Ox, 118

P

Pagoda, 129, 130
Paisley, 144
Palm tree, 136
Perle cotton, 181
Persian yarn, 181, 184, 185
Pinwheels, 53
Punch-and-stab stitching, 182

Q

Queen, 104, 108-109

R

Rabbit, 72, 119
Ram, 62, 128
Religious designs, 81-102
Rooster, 9, 19
Rug yarn, 185

S

Saint Peter, 178
Satin stitch, diagonal, 190
Scorpion, 64
Scotch stitch, 190
    alternating, 191
    checkerboard, 190
    diagonal satin, 190

outlined, 190
Scroll, 96
Seashells, 151
Seasons, 76-79
Sheep, 69, 70, 87, 92, 124, 163
Shepherds, 70
Ship, 91, 95
    Noah's ark, 98
    oriental, 130
Signs of the zodiac, 60-64
Slanted encroaching gobelin stitch, 190
Slanted gobelin stitch, 190
Sleigh, 79
Smyrna cross stitch, 189
Snake, 123
Snowflakes, 76, 145, 150
Stained glass windows, 81, 97, 154
Stars, 59, 67, 74-75, 79
Stem stitch with backstitching, 190
Stitches
    cross stitch, 181, 182
    needlepoint, 188-191
Sunbonnet babies, 48, 53
Sword, flaming, 84

T

Tablet, 96
Tapestry yarn, 185
Temples, 129, 130, 135
Tent stitch, horizontal and vertical, 188
    diagonal, 188
Thanksgiving, 73
Thread, for cross stitch, 180-181
Threading the needle
    cross stitch, 181
    needlepoint, 185-186
Tic-tac-toe board, 112
Tigers, 122-123, 125
Tree, 130
Triangle stitch, 191
Turkey, 73

U

Unicorn, 58
Upright cross stitch, 189
Upright gobelin stitch, 190

W

Wave, 133
Wedding announcement frame, 80
Wheat, 82
Windmills, 135
Working from a charted design, 176-177
Woven stitch, 191

Y

Yarns, 181, 184-185